Cori

Sources of Significance

Dear
Matt,
Great talking
with you

Corey

Philosophy/Communication
Ramsey Eric Ramsey, Series Editor

Sources of Significance
Worldly Rejuvenation and Neo-Stoic Heroism

By Corey Anton

Purdue University Press
West Lafayette, Indiana

Library of Congress Cataloging-in-Publication Data

Anton, Corey.
  Sources of significance : worldly rejuvenation and neo-stoic
heroism / Corey Anton.
      p. cm. -- (Philosophy/communication)
  Includes bibliographical references (p.   ) and index.
  ISBN 978-1-55753-561-0
  1. Ethics. 2. Conduct of life. 3. Stoics. 4. Becker, Ernest. 5.
Heroes--Psychology. 6. Self-esteem. I. Title.
  BJ37.A57 2010
  171'.2--dc22
                              2010003106

*For his insight and inspiration
I dedicate this work
to my early mentor,
Lee Thayer*

Table of Contents

ACKNOWLEDGMENTS

I need to thank Grand Valley State University (GVSU) for the sabbatical leave that enabled the production of the bulk of this work. Without such generous support and release time from teaching duties, this book would not exist. As I have presented small parts of this work over the past several years at various conferences, I would like to express thanks to the Media Ecology Association as well as the National Communication Association, including its Semiotics and Communication Division, the Rhetorical and Communication Theory Division, and the Kenneth Burke Society. These venues have given me space, time, and collegiate feedback and have greatly helped to settle the present ideas into their existing form.

Many people have helped me think about these ideas over past twenty years. I want to acknowledge friends with whom I have discussed these ideas at length, in particular Barry D. Liss, Bryan Wehr, and Abe Zakhem. I want to thank Phil Paradowski for reading passages of *The Wisdom of the Sands* aloud in his dorm room back in 1990. I also wish to acknowledge and thank my master's thesis committee members, Mary Anne Moffitt, John Cragan, and David Baldwin. I want to thank my colleagues and students at GVSU, especially Robert Mayberry, who introduced me to the works of Hans Jonas. Other colleagues at GVSU who I have talked with and gained ideas along the way include: Dewey Hoitinga, Barry Castro, John Drabinski, Allen Whipps, Mark Pestana, and Steven Rowe. For editorial assistance in the final stage I wish to thank Jermaine Martinez, Brett Lyszak, John Dowd, Denyse Seiler, Patrick Millard, and Barry D. Liss. I also want to thank Valerie V. Peterson for her love and support, for countless discussions, for her extensive suggestions, and for all of her useful editing assistance at various stages.

Lastly, I want to thank the Estate of Kenneth Burke for the kind permission to reprint Burke's poem "The Dialectician's Hymn." And I also wish to gratefully acknowledge Bill Watterson for the permission to reprint the cartoon from "Calvin and Hobbes."

PART I
LOGOS, NATURAL GUILT, AND THE HUMAN CONDITION

Marie Becker remarks about Ernest,
now dying, saying that he had
"…no energy remaining in him
for any further barter with the gods."
(Becker 1975, xv)

"The infantile conflict
between actual impotence
and dreams of omnipotence
is also the basic theme
of the universal history of mankind."
(Norman O. Brown 1985, 25)

CHAPTER 1

FROM SELF-ESTEEM TO THE MODERN CAUSA SUI PROJECT

Who has not pondered over the fireball that illuminates the daytime sky? Countless people across the globe and throughout history have looked to it and wondered about it. Many people have even worshipped it. Scientists today tell us that everything on this planet feeds off of the sun directly through photosynthesis or indirectly by absorption or ingestion. Try to remember this the next time you are eating a piece of fruit, a bit of light-ripened flesh. You also may want to wonder, "What exactly does it mean to be an eater?" Eating, if we want to be honest about it, is death consumption, at least that's what a good number of myths suggest. Snakes, because they shed their skin, mythically symbolize life's ability to cast off death. Posed in a circle and shown eating the very "death" that it sloughs off, the mythic snake image represents the fact that life feeds on its own mortality. Death is the way that life eats itself. Life plus death equals food. But the circle of life and death on this planet is possible and in fact remains visible only because it comes from what, properly speaking, was not born and does not die: the fire in the sky.

Other questions soon follow. Looking down at our hands we may ask: "Whose are these? And…What is all of this? *Where* is it? Where did it all come from?" The questions posed here are not threadbare, not "why is there something rather than nothing?" They regard something else, something that needs our concerted attention: the emergence of self-consciousness, the pangs of conscience, and the awareness of death—in a word, the entire world of *meaning*. And, the more that we are without any solid response to fundamental questions regarding our own origin, nature, and ultimate ends, the easier it seems to further ask: Does any of this matter? Does life ultimately mean anything? An ironic and morose response to these questions is that "meaning," "conscience," or "the significance of life" are outdated fantasies or relics from earlier days. A person's life can be boiled down to worm food. But even on its own terms such an account would be too reductive and final, for in our hair follicles reside countless microscopic organisms. We cannot wash them off, and apparently, this parasitic relationship has unidentifiably ancient origins. We are, therefore, much more than worm food when we die. At the very least, we are edible homes all the way along. To be alive is to be a site for living.

There is something else too. As living and breathing organisms take on the dimension of inner individuation by way of symbols and extended self-reflection, they become fundamentally unsure of how they fit (or should fit) with everything else. They come to stick out as if in relief from all else, and they inevitably concern themselves with issues such as: How, in what ways, to whom, is life (mine or others) ultimately significant or relevant? Ambiguities abound, and here the questions and responses regarding death and its relation to the meaning of life call for sustained address. Humanity, in so many of its forms, pursues such questions and/ or dwells in the response to them.

The Contributions of Ernest Becker

This chapter addresses the meaning of death and life as well as outlines the sources of significance by focusing upon the works of Ernest Becker, a key figure in death/life studies.[1] Few scholars are as accessible, as provocative, or as relevant to these issues. Becker's work also stands out because of his textual persona. He manages to convey what his scholarship identifies as the most vital of human needs: *unmistakable conviction and a sense that meaningful self-understanding is possible.*

What makes Becker's orientation so outstanding is his solid grasp of the problems ushered in during the age of great disillusionment. The combination of Enlightenment thought, anthropological studies, as well as the works of Darwin, Freud, and Marx had successfully pulled back the curtain on culture. Modernity came to see cultures as fictions and came to grasp the arbitrariness of cultural practices in ways that earlier peoples did not. As Becker suggests, "The most astonishing thing of all, about man's fictions, is not that they have from prehistoric times hung like a flimsy canopy over his social world, but that he should have come to discover them at all" (1971a, 139). Today we live in the wake of that discovery; we are more aware than ever before of the possibilities of grand-style self-delusion.

Becker, not surprisingly, wanted solid grounding for his ideas. He started from the fact that humans are animals and in this regard are similar to all other animals on the planet. They are subject to basic needs, and eventually, they die. But unlike so many other scholars who begin there, Becker's naturalism makes room for theological dimensions of life. Cultures per se, he argued, are inevitably religious institutions; they are systems that promise meaning beyond the sheer materiality of biological death. This means that any naturalism needs to acknowledge that theological speculation has provided some of the most creative responses to the ultimate mysteries of existence and it also has spoken to the whole of reality as humans experience it. Said point blank: *Humans are organisms of transcendence, and this is the biological fact.* We have a biological drive toward self-definitions that expand to epic and cosmic proportions. For these reasons—and more that become apparent throughout this chapter—Becker's work gives an excellent point of departure.

As author, he appears as a prophetic scholar returning from deep study to confidently proclaim long-awaited insights regarding humanity's nature and possible future. To illustrate, consider the introduction to his *Beyond Alienation*, where Becker writes, "...after one hundred and fifty years of groping we are at last in a position to offer what we have always wanted, but could not in modern times achieve...the authentic solution that has taken shape in our time, and can now be offered for discussion to the intelligent public at large" (1967, x).[2] In the second edition of his *The Birth and Death of Meaning*, Becker suggests that, "probably the most thrilling and potentially liberating discoveries have been made in the fields of anthropology, sociology, psychology, and psychiatry. The result is that we are today in possession of an excellent general theory of human nature, and this is what I want to reveal to the reader" (1971a, vii). This same prophetic urgency can be found in *The Denial of Death* (1973)—which won Becker the Pulitzer Prize. Arguing that Marxist and Freudian followers have adequately grown together—each pruned and cultivated by the other—Becker claimed that we have arrived "at the potentially most liberating question of all, the main problem of human life" (ibid., 1; 6). He argues that the urgent tone of the book is justified by the fact that "everyone is carrying on as though the vital truths about man did not yet exist" (ibid., 8). In summary, Becker believed that two centuries of research in psychology, psychiatry, education, anthropology, and sociology have made possible a comprehensive understanding of humanity, and this was the massive task he took upon himself. He tried to synthesize, integrate, and make publicly available scientific findings regarding the nature of the human.

As his own life was prematurely coming to an end, Becker increasingly recognized shortcomings in his earlier orientation and began to question some of his initial assumptions. In his final writing, published posthumously and against his wishes, we find the earlier optimism all but dried up. Tone still urgent as ever but increasingly grim, Becker's final writing casts a sobering if not downright disheartening account of humanity's history and likely future. In the preface to *Escape from Evil*, for example, he suggests that at this point in his career (as he nears the end of his flagging struggle against cancer) he finally has the courage to more thoroughly appraise humanity, including its darker sides. He suggests that his "concluded pessimism" is drawn from the scientific findings available.[3] He states, "My writings did not take sufficient account of the truly vicious human behavior," and he maintains that his pessimistic conclusion is not idiosyncratic, but rather reflects ideas that were, "gathered by the best minds of many dispositions and epochs…it reflects objectively the universal situation of the creature we call the human" (1975, xviii).

All said, Becker began his scholarly career by enthusiastically announcing long-awaited discoveries regarding the human condition only to be soured at the end. The questions I want to address are: what were the vital truths Becker first thought held the possibilities of bringing about ultimate relevance and liberation, and why did his diagnosis and prognosis change so sharply? Furthermore, how might his overall project be salvaged? To these questions I now turn.

First, Becker's sketch of humanity stands out not merely because of its clarity, relevance, and many useful insights, but because we now can see the development and progression in his thought. We can explore how and where small differences in focus and emphasis would have led to very different conclusions. And so, in response to the first question regarding vital truths about humanity, Becker introduces a host of concepts that range from "organismal anxiety," "self-esteem," and "characterology" to "heroism" and "death denial" to "natural guilt," "rituals of expiation," and "the causa sui project." Early in his mature thought, in the second edition of *The Birth and Death of Meaning*, Becker began by casting self-esteem as the central motive underlying human psychology, personality development, and cultural forms. Such self-esteem develops through cultural symbol systems and quickly culminates into a bid for heroism and death denial. Nevertheless, the notion of self-esteem remained too abstract for Becker; it failed to provide the kind of unified theory for motivation that he once believed it did. By *Escape from Evil*, Becker came to grasp how cultures, as "styles of heroic death denial," were tangled into processes of guilt expiation that can, and often do, take the form of "scapegoating" and "sacrifice." On the one hand, Becker came to grasp how humans kill, not as a result of instinctual aggression nor merely as vented frustration, but because it furnishes a sense of meaning. On the other hand, he also came to see how dwarfed and impoverished is the meaning horizon of contemporary consumer capitalism—a world of distraction and petty self-flattery, meaning horizons that boil down to serving oneself in a wholly secular or mundane plane.

And what about the second question? Why did his views change so drastically? Becker himself gave to posterity a call to reconsider his ideas. In the preface to *Escape from Evil* he seems to invite response to his own intellectual developments and progressions where he writes:

> Obviously it is an enormous problem: to show that man *is* truly evil- causing in much of his motivations, and yet to move beyond this to the possibilities of sane, renewing action, some kind of third alternative between bureaucratic science and despair. Whether I have succeeded in leaving open the possibility for such a third alternative, while looking man full in the face for the first time in my career, is for others to say…it would be easy for any interested student to trace—if he had the inclination to—the errors and wanderings, the inevitable record of personal growth and sobering that characterizes a so-called scientific life. (1975, xviii)

Accordingly, chapter 1 of the present study attempts to appraise and develop Becker's ideas. I begin by first reviewing the essence of "self-esteem," "self-esteem pursuit," and his notion of "psychoanalytic characterology." I then show how these, by way of cultural fictions, culminate into heroic death denial. Finally, using the main ideas of *Escape from Evil*, where all societies are cast as offering "styles of heroic death denial," I suggest that self-esteem, heroism, and even "death denial" can be viewed as smaller elements within two more unified phenomena, centerpieces for Becker's final writing: natural guilt and the casua sui project.

In its entirety, then, this book is offered as a sustained response to the questions surrounding the salvageability of Becker's project as a whole. Of the ten books that Becker authored, I draw mainly upon his final three, considering these to be his mature works. They are the second edition of *The Birth and Death of Meaning* (1971), *The Denial of Death* (1973), and *Escape from Evil* (1975).[4]

The Self-Esteem Motive

Of all the concepts that could be offered to initiate a discussion about motives and the human condition, self-worth comes first on the list. If we are disinclined to give self-worth such primacy, this is partly because self-esteem very recently has become synonymous with self-indulgence, feel-goodism, or egotistical self-pandering. Such sensibilities receive comic portrayal in the following "Calvin and Hobbes" cartoon.

Popular Conceptions of the Self-Esteem Motive

Intelligible to millions, this cartoon illustrates how self-esteem popularly aligns with vanity, self-indulgence, and/or petty self-flattery. People find such cartoons funny because they recognize that the "need for self-esteem" quickly slides into delusional pursuits of self-gratification. Despite these obstacles, I intend to show that we nevertheless can distinguish, extricate, and salvage an understanding of the basic human need for self-worth.

The importance of self-worth becomes more apparent if we consider our early infancy. In our earliest days, we achieved a sense of well-being and felt that all was right in the world if only we received adequate feeding, attention, and affection. Such acts quelled our organismal anxieties and supplied a growing sense of command over the world. The sense of self-esteem grew as mastery over body and environment increased, and it is here, precisely, that the centrality of self-esteem starts to become more apparent. Self-esteem can thus be understood, as Becker writes, as

> a natural systematic continuation of the early ego efforts to handle anxiety; it is the durational extension of an effective anxiety-buffer. We can then see that the seemingly trite words "self-esteem" are at the very core of human adaptation…The qualitative feeling of self-value is the basic predicate for human action. (1971a, 67)

Pleasures, gratifications, senses of well-being—especially when willfully obtained—effect a sense of autonomy and feed the sense of self-esteem, which then further builds up the prerogative to act. Even something so simple as the act of standing in an upright posture is a tremendous feat, a self-esteem building accomplishment.[5] But if this were the highest stage of phylogenic development humans attained, the fuller needs for self-esteem would not come to bloom. Nor would we have sufficient warrant for deeming self-esteem as central to the human condition.

Humans not only suffer anxiety regarding their ability to satisfy desires and obtain immediate goals; they are self-aware organisms who understand the world mainly through symbols and language. Part of the challenge, then, is to think openly and honestly about the relations between self-conscious organisms and their environments and to be ready to address how both self and world are subject to an unending ebb and flow of symbolic expansions and contractions. For Becker, this means de-sexualizing Freud's Oedipus complex, and in its place we find the painfully confusing transition from a biological creature to an increasingly symbolizing and symbolized one.[6] This challenging transition is made possible by parental imposition or blocking. In time, children learn how to say "no" to their own bodily and immediate gratifications, and they develop other avenues of satisfaction, particularly symbolic avenues. They learn, for example, to refrain from running through the flowerbed, chasing the kitty, or playing with mashed potatoes. Characterizing this traumatic early transition from animality to symbolicity, Becker writes:

> ...self-value no longer derives from the mother's milk but from her mouth. It comes to be derived from symbols...Once this has been achieved the rest of the person's entire life becomes animated by the artificial symbolism of self-worth; almost all his time is devoted to the protection, maintenance, and aggrandizement of the symbolic edifice of his self-esteem. (1971a, 67)

Self-esteem henceforth becomes invested into parentally-sanctioned practices and beliefs. Moreover, when symbols become the bulk of food for feeding self-esteem, the need for recognition can become limitless and the measures can be finely nuanced. Few situations fail to hold opportunities for maintaining, gaining, and/or losing self-esteem. Toddlers pull upon pant legs and routinely proclaim, "Look at me! Look at me!"[7] They ask, "Why did you give her four candies and me only three?" Envy and jealousy, products of the recognition that value is not bestowed equally, are therefore predictable features of a symbolically loaded drive to self-esteem. Obviously then, if youngsters were not self-aware the question of equal or fair treatment would be moot. As it is, though, children have some sense how they are valued—how they are relevant—and to what degree.

But self-worth is not merely placed upon us from the outside: we come to internalize a sense of self. We self-reflexively manage it even when all alone. We internally play what Becker calls an "inner-newsreel." We rehearse and view over again and again those images, scenes, and vignettes that bear upon our sense of self-worth. We may play back a witty comment we made, or reflect on how thoughtful everyone said we were. We can anticipate making a perfect remark on some future occasion. We may even imagine how future performances or accomplishments will be valued, and this value then seems to justify the drive toward them. On the other hand, we may relive our humiliations, inadequacies, or moments of embarrassment. We can obsess over a poor performance or over the possibility of one. By way of the inner-newsreel, self-worth is almost constantly self-indicated. And, because it is possible to live fictions as if they were not fictions, the sense of self-worth may telescope outward to cosmic proportions or burst into shards and dust.

To summarize so far, we first considered the fact of organismal anxiety-buffering and then explored how symbols and symbolically-imbued practices expand and contract the sense of self-worth. Although the roots of self-esteem are to be found in organismal desires and anxiety buffers, it is symbolic self-consciousness that precipitates expanding and contracting senses of self-worth. Becker situates these developments as part of a grand evolutionary culmination:

> Once you took the general instinct of self-preservation of the lower animals, the basic irritability of protoplasm, the self-identity of the physio-chemistry, the vague pulsation of the world of the animal's inner processes, the nameless feeling of power and satisfaction in carrying out his instinctive behaviors—once you took all this and gave it a directive self-control via ego, and a precise, symbolic designation in a world of symbols, then you resulted in nothing less than the need for heroic self-identity. (1971a, 76-77)

It is culture, we shall see, that does precisely this. Culture provides a massive codified system of rituals and symbolic practices, all issuing and maintaining various levels of worth and value. Personality and cultural form are revealed to be two aspects of the same thing: both are horizons for maintaining various modes of self-worth.

Psychoanalytic Characterology: Cultural Roles and Status

All cultures must secure for their members the material means for survival, but it would be unwarranted to conclude that culture provides nothing more than this or even is primarily about this. Moreover, personality is not a raw expression of inner character traits or innate behavioral dispositions. Both of these realms, culture and personality, are basically ongoing rituals and symbolic performances for producing and sustaining senses of self-worth. "One crucial function of culture," writes Becker, "is to make *continued* self-esteem possible. Its task, in other words, is to provide the individual with the conviction that he is *an object of primary value in a world of meaningful action*" (1971a, 79). People may be embarrassed to have their actions reduced to such motives; it is unsettling to discover worldviews and personality types as fictions constructed largely for the ends of sustained self-esteem. And so, if we remain reluctant to give self-esteem such centrality, we might benefit by further exploring how personality and cultural forms merge in the pursuit and maintenance of self-esteem.

Becker offers the term "psychoanalytic characterology" to identify how different personality types, codified and standardized by symbols and ritual performances, repress their origins, nature, and underlying goals. He thus agrees with Freud that people repress what they really are up to, but he disagrees regarding what is being repressed. For Freud it was Eros (the sex drive) and Thanatos (the death drive). For Becker it is the drive toward heroic self-worth. Subjected to psychoanalytic characterology, then, personality types can be disclosed as symbolic and highly stylized routes for pursuing and managing self-esteem. The bewildering array of cultural practices, social forms, customs, rules, and rituals, all with their corresponding entitlements, proscriptions, prescriptions, and various codes of propriety, give material form to a symbolic (that is, an expanded though fragile) sense of self-worth.

This means that even the most basic cultural symbols, personal names, are not simply verbal conveniences, nor can their function be reduced to indexing self and other. Names make us stand out in relief from all else. They make us unique but never wholly unrelated. For example, names, both first and last, are commonly "kept in the family" so that ancestors and relatives commonly share in them. Someone might be named after a great uncle, be the third generation "William," or take another's last name in marriage. These basic symbolic identifications extend and expand the sense of organismal boundaries, and they also precipitate new demands, challenges, obligations, and opportunities for self-worth.

But self-esteem blazes up not merely by identifications with personal names. Children also are taught the names of things around them.[8] They are taught how to speak about things and how things are to be valued. They also are told about their family history and traditions, about their community and the larger world. Additionally, they are taught about what is good and what is bad, what is to be done and what is to be avoided. "And, as soon as one course of action becomes 'right' and another 'wrong,'" writes Becker, "life becomes moral and meaningful. Morality is…a prescription for choice,…'meaning' is born as the choice is carried into action" (1971a, 79). Events of everyday life increasingly take meaningful form as people are able to take deep vested interests in their practices and worldviews. It is also worth underscoring that in our early years, interactions with the larger anonymous world are highly limited, if not nearly nonexistent. This sheltering allows for substantial development of both a sense of self-worth and an authorized worldview including its implied moral order. Many children, not having to face the anonymity and moral complexities of the larger social world, experience a world that is largely confirming.[9] Removed from the continued threat of utter irrelevance or views that could threaten the moral-authority assumed by the parents, children become vitally attached to systems of cultural symbols and their corresponding values and perspectives. Whether by kindhearted generosity, athletic prowess, academic achievement, artistic talents, wit, good looks, popularity, wealth, or other means, children and young adults learn to esteem themselves in ways that are culturally delineated. These competencies and characteristics, always strewn with symbols and ritual forms, become a kind of "character armor" that enables people to fend off challenges to their self-worth.

A humorous image from popular culture is of a person standing before a mirror, telling himself, "I'm good enough, I'm smart enough, and doggone it, people like me!" Part of what makes this funny is that direct attempts to self-worth are self-defeating. The comical image depicts a modern day rendering of Hegel's master/slave dialectic; it impresses upon us how self-worth cannot found itself. It cannot be a gift that we bestow upon ourselves, for the economy is too insular.[10] Only by something outside of ourselves (transcendent horizons, actual others, skills, objects, or events well cared-over) can we give breadth and depth and life to our self-worth. For self-esteem, we rely upon what is outside the self.

Self-worth and conviction increasingly run together as a person's worldview gives direction and order to his or her life projects. But this also suggests that self-conscious employment of symbols renders humans incapable of straightforward action, and, understood as such, what is commonly identified as "ethnocentrism" includes a wider circumference than simple self-interest. Said otherwise, because we could be absolutely wrong regarding who we are and how we are to be valued, we stave off this supreme terror by taking refuge in deep conviction. What is involved is nothing less than a cultural "re-instinctivization." Molded and solidified by cultural forms deeply infused, personality emerges only after acculturation sets in; people simply find their beliefs, values, and practices to feel natural.

Heroic Death Denial

Culture provides a codified hero-system that enables its members, some more than others, to maintain a sustained and validated sense of primary value in a world of meaningful action. All cultures, whether explicitly acknowledged as such or not, are inherently religious; they provide form and structure for human transcendence. As Becker writes, "culture itself is sacred, since it is the 'religion' that assures in some way the perpetuation of its members…all systematizations of culture have in the end the same goal…to assure them that in some ways their lives count in the universe more than merely physical things count" (1975, 4). All cultures create ritual forms that enable members to symbolically transcend their sheer materiality and organismal being, but cultural forms not only extend organismal boundaries and amplify routes for the pursuit of self-esteem, they also whet the appetite for some kind of immortality.

Cultural forms provide the promise of heroic victory over the demise of the flesh. One example already mentioned is names. Names typify the human desire to go other than the way of the insect's nameless, faceless, and unremembered death. Most people don't symbolically individuate the bugs they are about to squash, and this offers a clue to the meaning of naming and to the kind of transcendence a name can bestow. With names, we become more than our material bodies; we can be invoked when we are not there or even after our passing.

We are, Becker suggests, an ambiguity of both animal and spirit, and this irresolvable ambiguity fills us with dread. Finding psychology and religion to merge in the works of Kierkegaard, Becker writes, "Man's anxiety is a function of his sheer ambiguity and of his complete powerlessness to overcome that ambiguity, to be straightforwardly an animal or an angel" (1973, 69). We undoubtedly are animals, beings who have evolved through natural evolution and are akin to other animals as far as materiality and mortality are concerned. On the other hand, we experience freedom, choice, and transcendence, and because of our involvements within symbolicity, we have the capacity, if only partially and ambiguously, to span far and wide in our sense of self, including contemplation of ultimate ends.

The drive of self-esteem thus begins as an organismal anxiety-buffer, but as it is fed and cultivated through countless symbols and ritual practices, its demands expand exponentially. The drive of self-worth seems to know no limits and yet the bid for ultimate worth faces the ultimate obstacle: death. Death confronts and challenges any claim to ultimate meaning. And so, the phenomenon of death denial can be understood as part of the drive toward self-esteem; it is the natural perfection of the self-esteem motive.

To be socialized is to participate in various cultural dramas that ritually enact power over the forces of life and death, and all cultures everywhere can accordingly be examined, comparatively, as "*styles of heroic death denial*" (cf. Becker 1975). Such comparative study looks at how different cultures provide means for heroic death denial and then assesses respective costs of the hero-systems. "These costs," Becker suggests, "can be tallied roughly in two ways: in terms of the tyranny practiced within the society, and in terms of the victimage practiced against alien or 'enemies' outside it" (1975, 125). Said simply, so much of the hell on earth today comes from people wanting to be "special," people wanting a worldly paradise for themselves, or personal immortality, or simply wanting to rid the world of what they believe is evil.

Evil, on the contrary, comes about from people trying to escape from all paths toward death. Here the term "death" does not refer to the fact of biological cessation. It is, on the contrary, a kind of meta-symbol, a synecdoche for weakness, sickness, disease, impotence, frailty, fragility, finitude, and utter meaning-lessness. Forms of racism, sexism, and fascism as well as religious crusades and militant nationalisms, all of these are part of the "character armor" people use in their attempts to secure ultimate meaning in the face of finitude. In a largely secular world, personal wealth seems to give the final promise for immortality: not only can some people acquire bulletproof glass, better security fences, and access to the best health care, they also can bestow their wealth upon generations of progeny.

The claim I am advancing here is not that all attempts at meaning are evil or even result in evil. It is that a large amount of the evil that humans do comes from someone striving for meaning, someone or some group attempting to be signifi-cant, important, beyond the horizon of finitude.[11] People commonly reduce others to sheer animality while claiming to be beyond it personally. In his final interview Becker states, "All the missiles, all the bombs, all human edifices are attempts to defy eternity by proclaiming that one is not a creature, that one is something spe-cial" (2005, 220). The humanly significant and all-important social question then becomes: what are the available horizons of meaning that are least destructive but that do not trivialize or impoverish the need for human self-worth? More on that later and throughout the rest of this work, but for more immediate purposes, I need to review how evil often comes from heroic death denial.

Some evil stems from ethnocentric or nationalistic identification with cul-tural beliefs and values, for example, the claim that one is of "the chosen people." People join gangs, hordes, or the war machine, and their lives take meaning from marching in lines and from losing themselves into something vaster than them-selves. Fetishizing good and evil within highly circumscribed cultural blinders and furnishing self-worth through comparative degradation of others, people commonly insulate themselves from others by rigidifying adherence to cultural and symbolic values. Countless examples, ancient and modern, can be given of how collective identifications reify ideologies and serve the ends of discrimina-tion, degradation, exploitation, and even collectivist extermination.

The ability to vanquish a formidable foe, as if demonstrating the power to dispense life and death, shows power over death. In fact, it is not uncommon for people to feel powerful simply by watching something die at someone's hands. Drawing upon ample historical and social evidence, Becker argues that many people, perhaps more than we would like to admit, gain a sense of pleasure from taking life and/or watching others in misery. By lording over and watching others in a display of dying, people can feel the power of life and death as wielded by human hands.

We need to come to terms, argues Becker, with the long history of scape-goating. The scapegoat, as sacrificial vessel, is heaped with evils that are to be cast out, and then the vessel is either run out of the community or torn to shreds in the cult of the kill. Such forms of sacrifice are often practiced as attempts to generate power. The Nazi's "death potlatch" attempted nothing less than creating power by heaping death upon death, hoping to make power circulate. Power seems most aligned with those who dispense the power of life and death. People thus try to purge and purify the world of evil, but this can never be, for death is at the very heart of our being. It is part of who we are, not some thing in the world that could be blotted out by a form of cultural heroism.

Becker's encounter with the works of Otto Rank cast a significant influence over his thought during his final years. Rank, along with Norman O. Brown, helped to put both Freudianism as well as Rousseau into proper historical perspective. And Rank in particular, to whom *Escape from Evil* was dedicated, helped sober up Becker's thought. This sobering can be seen where Becker writes,

> If we add together the logic of the heroic with the necessary fetishization of evil, we get a formula that is no longer pathetic but terrifying. It explains all by itself why man, of all animals has caused the most devastation on earth—the most real evil. He struggles extra hard to be immune to death because he alone is conscious of it; but by being able to identify and isolate evil arbitrarily, he is capable of lashing out in all directions against imagined dangers of this world...the hero proves his power by winning in battle; he shows that he is favored by the gods. Also, he can appease the gods by offering to them the sacrifice of the stranger. The hero is, then, the one who accrues power by his acts, and who placates invisible powers by his expiations. (1975, 150)

This account of misdirected heroism marks a significant shift in focus. Whereas the earlier Becker stressed the self-esteem motive and how it related to heroic death denial, the later Becker recognized that this explanation was still too frag-mentary. The drive toward self-esteem and heroic death-denial increasingly came into focus as elements within a larger framework. We thus have arrived at the central problematic roughly sketched in *Escape from Evil*: a general theory of "natural guilt" and "guilt expiation."

Natural Guilt and Heroic Guilt-Expiation

The contemporary and common understanding of guilt refers to the experience of self-inflicted shame or remorse over some known wrongdoing. In fairly signifi-cant contrast to this, we can identify an ontological notion of guilt, one insepa-rable from the human condition.[12] In one of his final pieces, "The Spectrum of

Loneliness," Becker identifies what he calls *"the basic ontological motives of the human condition."* He writes,

> These motives are the familiar ones of Agape and Eros, the striving of man in two different directions…Under the impulsion of Agape, or sameness… The person feels lonely when he is different or apart, feels guilty for sticking out…Under the impulsion of Eros, or difference…the person…wants to stick out of nature as much as possible, be as unlike others as he can…This is the cause of the guilt that results from failing to develop oneself. Hence, the paradox which cannot be straightforwardly resolved. (2005, 232)

Natural guilt emerges, therefore, because we experience ourselves as both autonomous and individual as well as dependent and social. Total helplessness could be only a moment away—lives blown to ashes or suddenly washed under—but we nevertheless are independent entities who experience varying degrees of bodily-command and conscious self-sufficiency. Keeping this ambiguity in view, we can grasp how natural guilt is, as Becker suggests,

> a feeling of being blocked, limited, transcended without knowing why. It is the peculiar experience of an organism which can apprehend a totality of things and not be able to move in relation to it…Each person cannot stand his own emergence and the many ways in which his organism is dumbly baffled from within and transcended from without. (1975, 33; 35)

In sum, natural guilt emerges on two fronts: on the one hand, trying to cover-over how we depend upon the mysterious gifts of life, and on the other hand, recognizing that we have not adequately used our autonomy to give in return. "Guilt," Becker writes, "is a reflection of the problem of acting in the universe…It reflects the self-conscious animal's bafflement at having emerged from nature, at sticking out too much without knowing what for, at not being able to securely place himself in an eternal meaning system" (1975, 158).[13] These existential ambiguities also help to explain individuals' willing subordinacy to culture.[14] The experience of being cared-for makes such subordinacy a natural response. Furthermore, it is only as we grasp guilt in this ontological sense that we more fully understand the sacred nature of what today is regarded as "primitive" life.

Ritual practices of the earliest people were inherently spiritual gestures, heroic and sacrificial acts within tribal life. Such sacred enactments enabled cultural members to give back to the world, to appease its power, to feed and circulate and regenerate its flow, and to do so while safely tucked in the folds of social support. This is important because

> Society, in other words, is a dramatization of dependence and an exercise in mutual safety by the one animal in evolution who had to figure out a way of

appeasing himself as well as nature. We can conclude that primitives were more honest about these things—about guilt and debt—because they were more realistic about man's desperate situation vis-á-vis nature. (Becker 1975, 36)

Openly acknowledging their many debts and obligations, peoples of the earliest societies sought appeasement of the "invisible powers" from which their lives originated and upon which they continue to depend. Because they more clearly recognized (or more unabashedly admitted) their deep dependence upon the mysterious bounty of nature, earliest humans felt indebted and obligated to give in return. The origin of surplus, argues Becker, was a spiritual and not simply practical achievement: it originated as a sacrificial gift given to the invisible life-sustaining powers, and in so being, it structured and enabled perfect acts of both heroism and expiation.

> If we thus look at both sides of the picture of guilt, we can see that primitive man allocated to himself the two things that man needs most: the experience of prestige and power that constitutes man a hero, and the experience of expiation that relieves him of the guilt of being human. The gift complex took care of both these things superlatively. Man worked for economic surplus of some kind in order to have something to give...He protruded out of nature and tucked himself in with the very same gesture, a gesture of heroism-expiation. (1975, 36-37)

We can summarize by suggesting that humans need more than simply self-esteem or heroic death denial. First, because humans stick out and have cultivated a sense of self-sufficiency, they need to feel significant or in Becker's terms, "heroic."

Second, because people can "stick out too much," they need to adequately give in return so as to expiate the guilt of separation. In other words, people need to be identified with and recognize their dependence upon something vaster into which they can lose themselves. Here we are reminded of Odysseus's lesson regarding the all-too-human temptation: "Do not forget the gods; they are the source of life-sustaining powers." The more a person tries to escape from and/or deny dependency on the mystery, the more that

> this risks inflating him to proportions he cannot stand; he becomes too much like the gods themselves, and he must renounce this dangerous power. Not to do so is to be unbalanced, to run the great sin of *hubris* as the Greeks understood it. *Hubris* means forgetting where the real source of power lies and imagining that it is in oneself. (Becker 1975, 37)

It is precisely this temptation that was acceded to and advanced by the development of the "modern causa sui project." To address this development we first must address one of the key drifts that paved the way for its emergence: powerful and life-embodying personae and their relation to the origin and development of social inequality.

The ancient history of social inequality is not merely an account of guile and repressive powers of the few over the many. These factors are not to be denied, but adequate consideration must also be given to the ways that personal qualities served to bestow, at least in the minds of others, a sense of rank. Various persons came to dominate others not so much by physical coercion as by an aura of life-sustaining sacredness that others perceived in them. Others huddled to it and served it in the hopes of generating more life-sustaining power. The overall implication is that "Men are literally hypnotized by life and by those who represent life...*men fashion unfreedom as a bribe for self-perpetuation*" (1975, 51). The advancement of social inequality is thus caught in a history of the change from the invisible to the visible, the change from tribal hunting and gathering communities that were largely egalitarian to the centralizing and redistributive authority of a divine king. Divine kings emerged out of tribal life because members of the tribes, if only unconsciously, wanted a visible embodiment of life-sustaining power. This form, Becker suggests, is typified in the "Sun-Man," the person who symbolized all of the mystery, power, and life-sustaining force of the sun. Such concrete embodiment gave visible form to the mysterious and life-sustaining powers. It enabled people to feel closer to such life-sustaining power and seemingly gave the possibility of a kind of direct approval from the gods. It also allowed tribes to demonstrate power and wealth to their neighbors. As forms of collective strength, ritual practices made possible massive accumulations of surplus and gave awesome displays of life-generating power. Individuals, neatly stitched into the tribal fabric, could heroically challenge the omnipresent threats of existence while also enjoying the submersion and heroic cloak of cultural identifications. But the logic of surplus accumulation, which centralized wealth under a redistributive authority, seemingly sealed the fate of humanity to the motives and drives within the newly emerging tribal mana power: money.

Whereas earlier rituals of rejuvenation enabled both heroic and expiative meanings, consumer capitalism can be viewed as a degeneration of the heroic and expiative possibilities of earlier ages. In fact, Becker's depiction offers many insights into the ways that money (coupled with literacy and calendars) radically transformed the experience of natural guilt as well as altered the possibilities of guilt expiation.[15] Money, and all that it made possible, displaced the dominant and long-standing rituals of "gift-giving," led to the contemporary covering-over of natural guilt, and most generally funded the modern individual causa sui project. As Becker puts it:

Primitive man lived in a world devoid of clocks, progressive calendars, once-only numbered years. Nature was seen in her imagined purity of end- less cycles of sun risings and settings, moon waxings and wanings, seasons changing, animals dying and being born, etc. This kind of cosmology is not favorable to the accumulation of either guilt or property, since everything is wiped away with the gifts and nature is renewed with the help of ritual ceremonies of regeneration....[but] It could no longer be pretended that the ancient rituals of renewal could keep regenerating the city, and at this time growing numbers of people opted for Christianity, which promised the im- pending end of the world...No wonder the confusion of the ancient world was so great and tension and anxiety were so high: men had already amassed great burdens of guilt by amassing possessions, and there was no easy way to atone for this...This is how we understand the growth of the notion of "sin" historically. Theologically, sin means literally separation from the powers and protection of the gods, a setting up of oneself as a causa sui. (1975, 87-88)

Primitive rituals of regeneration sought to appease the gods and to ensure security and prosperity, as well as to ensure "right" relations to the invisible realm. In time people came to no longer engage in collective rituals for cosmic heroism and the appeasement of nature. On the contrary, human history is the tale of increasingly self-aware animals who would stop at nothing to remove their sense of depen- dency. Today, with the benefit of hindsight, we can see quite clearly that the bulk of the contemporary culture operates within the modern (i.e., individualist) causa sui project.

The Causa Sui Project: Natural and Modern

In traditional usage, the term "causa sui" referred only to the Divine, to the fact that the Divine does not depend upon anything else; it refers to that which is fully and completely (i.e., logically and/or temporally) the cause of itself. By the end of the nineteenth and twentieth centuries, the notion had become increasingly secularized and had grown into the ideas that Becker articulated in his final work. We might speculate that Becker was already familiar with Nietzsche's provoca- tion that:

The *causa sui* is the best self-contradiction that has been conceived so far, it is a sort of rape and perversion of logic; but the extravagant pride of man has managed to entangle itself profoundly and frightfully with just this nonsense. The desire for "freedom of the will" in the superlative metaphysical sense, which still holds sway, unfortunately, in the minds of the half-educated. The desire to bear the entire and ultimate responsibility for one's actions oneself, and to absolve God, the world, ancestors, chance, and society involves noth- ing less than to be precisely this *causa sui* and, with more than Munchausen's audacity, to pull oneself up and into existence by the hair, out of the swamps of nothingness. (Nietzsche 1968, 218)

Another of Becker's early influences, Sartre, poses a similar issue. The odyssey documented in his *Being and Nothingness* reveals how the "for-itself," as a lack, perpetually haunts the "in-itself" and culminates in the desire to surpass all desire. All of this, suggests Sartre, discloses human reality as the desire to be God. But if these ideas from Sartre and Nietzsche influenced Becker, they did not come into full focus until relatively late in his career, when he studied Brown's *Life Against Death*. In particular, it was Brown's understanding of the causa sui project, a Freudian interpretation whereby "causa sui" is equated with "the boy becoming the father of the man," that crystallized all the meanings above.

There are, according to Becker's final work, two basic kinds of causa sui in history. First is the original and "natural": the tribal and collectivist causa sui known under the name "culture." Culture in its totality offers humans the means to ensure meaningful action. Culture is a banding together in the struggle for meaningful survival, a collective effort that participates in countless regenerative rituals and gives reality to the notion that humans are not merely helpless animals facing their own utter dependency, finitude, and demise. Collective and tribal life, the brute and sheer fact of cultural time-binding, is the first and original event that marks the beginnings of the natural causa sui project.

The second kind of causa sui is the modern individualist kind. As much a cultural phenomenon as the first, it is a way that the first ended up developing itself. The modern causa sui project refers to the pervasive condition in which many people in modern Western cultures find themselves today. They believe in themselves as atomistic, autonomous, and isolated individuals. Secular individualist humanism and technologically-driven naturalism, both are aspects of the modern causa sui project. This means that individuals increasingly attempt to take themselves and experience themselves *as if they were of their own making.* Individuals increasingly feel as if they are or should be their own cause.

Living on a wholly secular plane, individuals today seek security and prosperity but almost exclusively in the visible world and mainly by having money in their hands. With accrued capital and accumulated material possessions, people lodge faith in themselves and think of themselves as being of their own making. In this regard, money has become the god of today (also cf. Needleman 1994). Money allows people to hold society itself in their hands and thus offers "*causa sui mana power.*" It is, as Becker suggests, the modern "totemic" possession. People so dedicatedly pursue money because it is the power of culture, the symbolic power of *self-sufficiency.* If money, as Kenneth Burke suggests, is "the symbol of symbols," and if, as Burke further argues, the love of money is the fullest exemplar of how humans attempt to escape their animality, then money is the "perfection" of the causa sui project. Becker summarizes his general position on this issue where he contrasts the above with the logic of ancient gift-giving that informed primitive rituals of worldly rejuvenation:

> Another way of putting this is to say that man has changed from the giving animal, the one who passes things on, to the wholly taking and keeping one. By continually taking and piling and computing interest and leaving to one's heirs, man contrives the illusion that he is in complete control of his destiny....Man imagines that the causa sui project is firmly in his hands, that he is the heroic maker and doer who takes what he creates, what is rightfully his. And so we see how modern man, in his one-dimensional economics, is driven by the lie of his life, by his denial of limitation, of the true state of natural affairs. If we sum it all up historically, we seem to be able to say that man became a greater victim of his drivenness when heroism pushed expiation out of the picture; man was now giving expression to only one side of his nature. He still needs expiation for the peace of his life because he is stuck with his natural and universal experience of guilt. (Becker 1975, 89-90)

All cultures naturally embody the causa sui project to some degree. The critical and distinguishing difference between the natural and modern causa sui project is that primitive cultures enacted *social* rituals for heroism and expiation (e.g., collective rituals of worldly rejuvenation and tribal gift-giving) whereas money and linear calendars began the heroic quest of *individualist* causa sui projects (e.g., private property, compound interest, and technological progress). This shift increasingly allowed individuals to think of themselves as of their own making and to think of their destiny as self-fashioned or chosen. All said, contemporary individualist consumer capitalism attempts to undercut the sense of natural guilt and perhaps deny it outright.

Historical Development of the Modern Causa Sui Project[16]

It was not exclusively money and calendars that brought about the full-scale individualist causa sui project that people experience today. Contemporary notions of the self-sufficient anonymous individual have emerged from and sustain themselves within numerous communication and transportation technologies, in particular the kinds of technologies made possible by alphabetic literacy. To better understand the individual casua sui project, then, we need to identify literacy as equally necessary and a partial contributor. We might say that money and literacy are the two legs upon which the modern casua sui project stands.

With money and alphabetic literacy to fuel them, functional individualist anonymity has bloomed and brought with it a growing range of products and services that enable the sense of self-sufficiency. We find more and more technologies of convenience, ease, and comfort, and on countless horizons, people today can purchase resources for dealing with nature only as they would like to appropriate it and on their own terms. They buy material conditions and technologies that enable them to avoid nature's intrusive disruptions and its overwhelming impositions. This also means that many "powerful" people today are less and less directly in contact with those aspects of existence that disclose natural guilt. That is, the consequence of the growth of such technologies has been that many people today may not recognize nor directly feel natural guilt. I offer three reasons to account for this.

First, life was, is, and most likely will remain, difficult. People face diseases, illnesses, natural disasters, hardships, suffering, and not only the unexpected deaths of others, but their own death as the ultimate limit of life. Such unpredictable and imposed-from-without blockages and limitations offer sites for mundane heroic struggle that may naturally expiate guilt. Adversity, struggle, labor, commitments, and sacrifices are the remnants of ritual routes of expiation indigenous to human life; these are still the homegrown fabrics by which most people stitch heroic meaning into their lives. This means that people who do not sufficiently labor for their money or who receive more than they deserve, or perhaps both, may have a sense of guilt, but if people work hard for their money and pay for things themselves, thinking "We have worked to earn our keep," they may feel there is nothing to "be guilty about." In summary of the first reason, the basic logic of "*laboring* to earn money," even if it is not regarded as such, operates as a natural form of guilt expiation.

Second, individuals may not feel a sense of natural guilt because they have fewer and fewer contacts where it is glaringly disclosed, and they now may attempt to hide from it. On many scales and in countless aspects of our lives, modern technologies (medical, industrial, practical, professional) have worked to eclipse and strategically cover the fact of our dependence on mysterious life-sustaining powers. Modern Western lives have become a kind of dramatic enactment that technologically dislocates people from situations that remind them of their dependence and humble place. Ever extending the boundaries of self-sufficiency, modern Western societies are a massive parade of *technological-heroism*.

Third, many people do not feel guilt today because modern technologies have thoroughly enabled the heroic and self-sufficient side of existence; this is Becker's one-dimensional economics. Countless developments such as increased life-expectancy, advances in medicine, and technological improvements are not to be denied outright. But still, if people come to think, as so many now do, that progress is a fact and not an ideology, they are basically practicing a religion, one which serves, if only round-aboutly, to deny natural guilt. Imagine someone believing the following: "One day technology will bring equality to everyone; all people will live in ease, security, and luxury." Such a narrative and its supporting beliefs may well be motivated by a desire to expiate guilt. Even if such a narrative does help to rationalize guilt away, is anyone really sure that such technological routes will effectively manage *natural* guilt? It is more likely the case that as technological progress continues, people increasingly make claims to expanded power and self-sufficiency, but these then become the ground for unintended consequences: "*Indignation*" becomes more and more frequent. When technologies break down, people often feel indignant rather than guilty. Breakdowns are taken not as disclosure of radical dependency. On the contrary, people seem to assume an entitlement to the engagements modern technologies make possible; they have expanded boundaries of self to include involvements made possible by the technologies. Here is just one illustration: The first automatic garage door opener was called a "Genie," perhaps because of its magical powers. Today, the magic is mostly gone. People have come to assume that the door opener will work and may attend to it only when it does not work. And, when it fails to work, "'*They*' ought to have made a better one" seems to be the quick and "indignant" conclusion, not, "Wow, I'm quite a presumptuous ingrate!" In summary, natural guilt is radically covered-over by the unending faith in technological progress, but the trouble is that the more "progress" people enjoy, the more thoroughly they can imagine their lives as self-sufficient, and the more they may suffer from a kind of indignation. See Figure 1.

Some Further Illustrations

Most people do not know the individuals who take their garbage away, if they have such services. Nor do they concern themselves with where it is dumped, unless, of course, it is too near to them. And garbage worker strikes? Nobody likes those. Although most people who have lived on this planet never experienced the ease and convenience known as "flushing the toilet," and many still do not, those who do have a toilet to flush try not to concern themselves with where the flush goes. People try not to think too much about their own excrement. But when people encounter an unflushed toilet marked "out of order," something more than a practical inconvenience seems to be occurring. It somehow becomes a window onto something the modern secular individualist would like to have forgotten.

Modern technologies have allowed full separation between the butchery of animals and what most people purchase as food. "Bacon, as found packaged in the supermarket," Alan Watts writes, "gives no intimation of pig, and steaks appear as if they were entities like apples, having no relation to the slicing of dead cattle" (1968, 42). How many people would eat meat if they personally had to

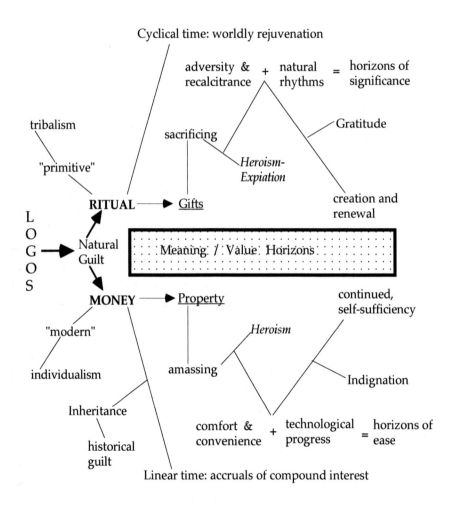

Figure 1. Schemata of basic differences between collectivist gift-giving culture and individualist consumer capitalist culture.

participate in the kill? How about if they merely had to witness the slaying of each animal from which they would eat? As modern consumers quickly exit a drive-thru and pull a cheeseburger from a bag, they may not think to say thanks to the origin of their food. They are actually more likely to complain that their food is not "done their way." Such radical disconnects between "food" and the plants and animals and processes behind the modern food industry may also be related to the steady decline of mealtime prayers. Would greater participation in and witnessing of animal slaughter not naturally increase inclinations toward prayers of expiation and thanks?

In many cities within the United States, for under $10, individuals can go into a buffet restaurant and dine upon a food assortment that rivals what only royalty had enjoyed throughout most of human history. At such establishments a person can consume what would be enough to feed a small family for several days, all for under the price of two hours' work at minimum wage. Interestingly, these god-like conditions serve not but to make possible the experience of indignation: "my burger is not warm enough and I said extra mustard!" or "their ice cream machine is 'out of order' and my steak is overdone!" or perhaps, "the plates are too small!" *Ad infinitum*. Who must people think they are?

Many modern homes in the United States come complete with climate controlled environments; regardless of outside temperatures, the air is conditioned or heated. Individuals can luxuriate in private hot tubs and can don a suntan year-round with a private tanning bed. For many if not most people, "contact with nature" is limited to parks, recreational areas, and nature preserves. Such dwindling contact with nature also can be seen in the loss of both diurnal and seasonal rhythms. People expect to have instant bright-lighting twenty-four hours a day, seven days a week. More and more stores and businesses now operate twenty-four hours a day, and supermarkets—also often open round-the-clock—increasingly have fruits and vegetables of all kinds regardless of season. On all these different fronts, spatially and temporally, the modern causa sui project has subdued the forces of nature.

Modern medical science has been perhaps the most successful in feeding the modern causa sui project. In *The Mature Society*, Nobel Laureate Dennis Gabor tells how the invention of morphine related to the end of public torture. The possibility of quelling pain made demonstrations of useless suffering appear as overly cruel. At this point in history, we have come a long way from ending public torture and seeking to alleviate human suffering. We have hair dyes and Rogaine, an increasing assortment of anti-aging drugs, numerous kinds of mood or attitude drugs, and many forms of reproductive/sexual technologies such as birth control, RU486, erectile dysfunction drugs, fertility drugs, and in vitro-fertilization.

Could there be any more obvious examples of the desire to be one's own cause? Well, yes, perhaps exemplified in cosmetic plastic surgery and designer genetic engineering. And finally, although there is not yet a cure for death, some people hope the day will come. Cryogenically frozen, they are waiting it out.

So many people seem to believe in technological progress in all aspects of life that they have come to assume the world does not vitally depend upon them to rejuvenate its resources. They fail to see that in many areas of life there cannot be collective progress. Many possibilities remain as possibilities only because certain individuals actively keep them open.

Where to Now?

Although they began with great optimism, Becker's mature works ended in pessimism. I suggest that it is mainly because he started with self-esteem as the basis of this theorizing and then only partly arrived at a theory of natural guilt that he felt betrayed by his earlier optimism. If Becker had begun with natural guilt as his cornerstone, perhaps he would not have grown so disheartened. The following is a more detailed account of these developments, one that tries to show why pessimism is not the only option.

Different sets of terms came into prominence for Becker at different points: "self-esteem," "ambiguity," "heroic death denial," and "natural guilt." Careful analysis reveals that all of these concepts are present throughout his final three books, and yet the order of their appearance roughly represents the order of predominance in his thinking. In *The Birth and Death of Meaning*, Becker still placed self-esteem and death denial within a fully organic and/or biological framework. But as his thought matured, he could no longer cast ambiguity as simply a threat to organismal integrity and something to be overcome; ambiguity took on a more expansive designation ("we are angels with anuses") and thus became a psychological and religious condition calling for continued ritual response. Near the end of the trilogy, self-esteem finally came into its clearest focus as part of natural guilt, and it is here that Becker began to comprehend the historical nature of the individual causa sui project. Consequently, he was able to identify self-esteem and death denial as remnants from and clues about the historical degeneration of rituals of cosmic rejuvenation. He also came to see the pivotal role that sacrifice played throughout human history and how earlier, primitive peoples differed from moderns in this regard. Acknowledging the long history of sacrifice and the ineradicability of guilt, Becker foresaw a grim future for humanity. He found nearly as dismal the demythologized consumer capitalist who is entrenched in the trivial one-dimensional heroism of personal wealth accumulation.

Adult members of traditional societies participated in countless ritual enactments that worked upon the invisible realm and thereby enabled heroic self-expansion into larger schemes of meaning. Becker minces no words on this subject where he suggests that primitive and traditional societies "could achieve even in the smallest daily task that sense of cosmic heroism that is the highest ambition of man" (1971a, 125-126). Early tribal peoples were able to engage in cosmic heroisms largely because their fictions were not yet debunked or unmasked. Few people today are able to take worldly regenerative rituals as other than superstitious delusions, and many people believe that cosmic senses of importance are quaint but misguided wishful thinking. "This is why modern man whines so pitifully with the burden of life," Becker writes, "he has nothing ultimate to dedicate it to; nothing infinite to assume responsibility for; nothing self-transcending to be truly courageous about. He has only himself, his dazzling and diverting little consumer objects; his few closely huddled loved ones; his live-span; his life insurance; his place in a merely biological and financial chain of things" (1967, 213). Indeed, in the wake of Freud, Marx, and Nietzsche, we are seemingly much more aware of the depths of human self-deception. But this is not to say that we do not cling to and huddle around our fictions just the same. We can grant that there is no returning to earlier innocence while still underscoring that people nevertheless need viable life-fulfilling mythologies to give form to their expiative-heroic enactments. Moreover, people need to grasp the cost of their heroisms and avoid the terrible significance offered by the military industrial complex on the one hand and the trivial and mostly indignant life-script of petty consumer capitalism on the other.

How might we find resources for basic life-strategies in Becker's work? How might we recover the gift-character of existence and also recognize the need for rituals of worldly rejuvenation?

First, we should address the genuine possibilities of the cosmological origins of the drive for self-worth. Like many other thinkers, Becker argues that the cosmos is in the gradual and inevitable process of increasing in degrees of freedom and individuation. Thus, in *The Denial of Death*, he strongly disagrees with the notion that humanity is a fluke or accident:

How can we say that evolution has made a mistake with man…The ego, on the contrary, represents…a step into a true kind of sub-divinity in nature…And… as far we can judge, a natural urge by the life force itself toward an expansion of experience, toward more life. (1973, 262-263)

The implication is that the drive to self-esteem, regardless of its distorted and flattened character in contemporary life, should not be dismissed as trivial and incidental self-absorbed vanity. Humans are much more than vain in their preoccupation with themselves; each and every person is in fact a part of all that is and all that ever will have been. Our bodies are fully of this universe, not merely some things that currently happen to be within it. Although people are never of their own making, humanity nevertheless is the place and moment of cosmic becoming where self-aware individuation becomes potent enough to generate natural guilt from the very success at this bid. By the potency of its powers for merger and division, life itself has carried us toward the agony of its own success at the causa sui project.

Second, Becker identifies one possible direction when he loosely calls for a kind of neo-Stoicism grounded in the extra-mundane heroism of death acceptance. He writes, "A creative myth is not simply a relapse into comfortable illusion; it has to be as bold as possible in order to be truly generative…daily life, then, becomes…a duty of cosmic proportions" (1973, 279). A neo-Stoical extra-mundane heroism, one that is grounded in death acceptance, does not bring about a miraculous transformation of the person or a sweeping transformation of the world. It does, however, open us to "new forms of courage and endurance" (1973, 279). It also motivates us against the pursuit of a personal afterlife and re-orients us toward other strategies of transcendence. In fully accepting death, life becomes the gift whereby we work for the eternal not only because it elevates and dignifies our efforts, but because it resonates with, amplifies, and enlivens the circulatory resources of the world. In a word: *we live not for our afterlife but for the existence of others as well as for the taste of eternity.* These are the ultimate resources to be explored in fuller detail.

In the next chapter, I try to make evident that Becker had not sufficiently grounded logos in the ambiguity of merger and division, nor had he explicitly made logos the ground for natural guilt. Accordingly, I need to provide a more robust account of logos, one that accounts for how logos and ambiguity relate, one that underscores how logos is a never ending tide of ambiguous merger and division.

Although many people have made contributions to such ideas, few are as relevant as Kenneth Burke. Becker admittedly cites Burke in two of his books, but he relies upon the ideas of Hugh Dalziel Duncan, one of Burke's students, in greater detail. If Becker had made Burke's work more central, he might have found resources for understanding logos as the ambiguity of merger and division, and for understanding how rich are the possibilities of "mortification" as the perfection of "sacrifice." He also might have found the means of reminding himself that the situation is not all that serious.[17] We can imagine that Burke might open his rejoinder with: "Let's not be overly earnest, Ernest."

Notes

1   Born in 1924 in Massachusetts, Becker joined the military, served in the infantry, and eventually, in his service, helped to liberate a Nazi concentration camp. After the service he attended Syracuse University and subsequently joined the U.S. Embassy in Paris. By the mid 1950s, he returned to Syracuse to pursue graduate work in philosophical anthropology. In subsequent years he taught at Upstate Medical Center at Syracuse where he developed a close relationship with Thomas Szasz, spent a year living in Rome, taught sociology at University of California, Berkeley, then social psychology at San Francisco State University, and finally joined an interdisciplinary department at Simon Fraser University in Vancouver. From 1961-1974, a mere thirteen years, Becker penned ten books and dozens of articles on meaning, alienation, aggression, self-esteem, death-denial, and the possibilities of sane education, all of which he took to be part of the relevant and enduring, though mostly underappreciated, aspects of Marx and Freud. Trying to integrate a full-on naturalism regarding human evolution with a robust sense of transcendent meaning horizons, he spent the bulk of his adult life attempting to formulate answers for why "people act the way they do" (cf. Becker, 2005).

2   Later in *Beyond Alienation*, Becker writes, "we actually solved that dilemma of all dilemmas, the most excruciating of all, the one that took the greatest toll of anguish in the best thinkers, the one the caused the most lofty geniuses to hem and hedge, the one that pitted mind against mind, book against endless book, during the whole history of modern thought" (1967, 162).

3   Becker admittedly makes a distinction between pessimism and cynicism. Liechty too (2005) identifies the second edition to *The Birth and Death of Meaning* as the turning toward more pessimism. At any rate, by the time Becker's *The Lost Science of Man* (1971b) was finally published, Becker grew increasingly aware that he would not see the grand unification of moral theory and sociology in his lifetime.

4   These three books are most recommended by The Ernest Becker Foundation.

5   Cf. "The Upright Posture" from *Phenomenological Psychology*.

6   Becker regards bed-wetting as an attempt of the body to reassert the primacy of the body over the symbolic realm.

7   Interested readers should see Idries Shah's "Characteristics of Attention and Observation," from *Learning How to Learn*.

8   As Helen Keller described in her memoir: "everything has a name and each name gave birth to a thought."

9   To suggest that this is confirming is not to suggest that it is favorable. Cf. R. D. Laing on "Confirmation and Disconfirmation" in *Self and Others*.

10 Cf. Lewis Hyde *The Gift*.

11 Few people set out to do evil or to live a life of crime. It happens mostly by complicity. The question is, why are people so willing? Kenneth Burke provides a rather interesting response. He writes, "Crime produces a kind of 'oneness with the universe' in leading to a sense of universal persecution whereby all that happens has direct reference to the criminal. There is no 'impersonality' in the environment; everything is charged with possibilities…And for the criminal, the whole world is thus purposive, so that the experience of criminal guilt in a sense restores the teleological view lost by evolutionism" (1962, 309).

12 Becker illustrates a wide range of experiences in which guilt becomes possible:

Man also experiences guilt because he takes up space and has unintended effects on others—for example, when we hurt others without intending to, just by being what we are or by following our natural desires and appetites, not to mention when we hurt others physically by accident or thoughtlessness...We feel guilt in relation to what weighs on us, a weight that we sense is more than we can handle, and so our...children are a burden of guilt because we cannot possibly foresee and handle all the accidents, sicknesses, etc. that can happen to them. We feel limited and bowed down, we can't be as carefree and self-expansive as we would like, the world is too much with us. If we feel guilt when we have not developed our potential, we are also put into a bind by developing too much. Our own uniqueness becomes a burden to us; we "stick out" more than we can safely manage. (1975, 33-34)

13 A few years earlier, Becker writes,

Today we understand that guilt is due to the human condition, the sense of being bound, overshadowed, feeling powerless. And we understand this guilt in these ways: in the sense that the body is a drag on human freedom, on the limitless ambitions for movement and expansion of the inner self. This is natural guilt, we might say; of course this is what Freud sensed and knew when he talked about the determinism of evolution and the trauma of birth and early experience, but it is hardly as specific as he wanted us to believe: it is not based on prehistoric events or on definite physical desires; it is rather a sense of futility, general limitation, and natural inferiority. Furthermore, as the existentialists have taught us, a person can even feel guilt in a relationship to the blockage of his own development: that he has not had the experiences or realized the urgings that seemed his natural right. We might say that a person can feel 'stifled' and beholden in relation to himself, to his own failed potential. (1971a, 63)

14 Becker writes, "Each person would literally be pulled off his feet and blown away or would gnaw away his own insides with acid anxiety if he did not tuck himself back into something. This is why the main general characteristic of guilt is that it must be shared: man cannot stand it alone..." (1975, 35).

15 An interesting point of debate regarding the usefulness of money as a horizon of significance comes from Eric Hoffer who suggests that money is an outstanding equalizer for the most widespread mundane heroism. He seems to agree with Becker regarding the need for self-worth (also cf. *The True Believer*), but he suggests that most people, lacking creative competencies, have come to rely upon the petty and easy heroism of monetary accumulationism. Hoffer writes,

The monstrous evils of the twentieth century have shown us that the greediest money grubbers are gentle doves compared with money-hating wolves like Lenin, Stalin, and Hitler, who in less than three decades killed or maimed nearly a hundred million men, women and children, and brought untold suffering to a large portion of mankind...What will life be like in a society without money? Men will try to assert and prove themselves by all sorts of means and under all sorts of conditions. This question is what means for demonstration of individual worth are likely to develop in a nonacquisitive society. Vying in creativeness is not a likely substitute for vying in acquisitiveness—not only because creativity is accessible to the relatively few, but because creative work is without automatic recognition and is not easily measured. Rather, the nonacquisitive society is likely to develop into a combination of army and school. People will prove themselves by winning degrees, medals and rank...A society without money will be largely preoccupied with managing people. There will be little social automatism. Sowing, harvesting, mining, manufacturing, etc. will become burning national problems. Instead of the harmless drug of money there will be the black magic of brainwashing and soul raping. Eventually the medicine men will be replaced by slave drivers. (1951, 37-39)

There is much truth here. We find a kind of harmony between Hoffer's and Becker's positions, at least insofar as they recognize that humans are self-reflexive and burdened with images of unattainable perfections, that is, partly motivated by the image they have of themselves. Still, Hoffer seems to mistake the outcome for the beauty of striving. There are few things more impoverished than a life that acts as if it is complete before it is. This work tries to show how money is necessary and inevitable, but remains rather limited in terms of its own horizons of significance. It offers relatively little transcendence per se, for it already is transcendence pure and simple.

16 I have identified natural guilt and the modern causa sui project as possibilities grounded in logos. The emergence of the individual—the self-conscious, reasoning person—out from animal submergence to the original "collective causa sui" known as culture, to this very high culmination of the culture that would be made of individuals is sketched as a kind of historical inevitability. In his *Man, the Measure*, Erich Kahler writes,

We have defined the human quality as man's overstepping of the limits of his own being, and have stated that it consists of two main acts, the establishment of these limits by detaching and discerning a non-self from a self, and the establishment of a new conscious relationship with the clearly conceived non-self by transcending self toward the non-self. History as the evolution of the human quality, then, is the *successive development of these two acts or faculties of man.* (1956, 18)

He further characterizes the drift from the collectivist causa sui to the modern project, he writes "Both processes of differentiation are a kind of focusing, a narrowing-down, in the one case, of a separate human mind or soul, as distinct from the universe, and in the other, of a separate individual as distinct from the human community" (1956, 18). Summarizing this progression Kahler writes,

The first period, from the condition of primitive man to the end of antiquity, comprises the process of man's detachment and discernment of an outer world from an inner world...The second period, from the end of antiquity to the Renaissance, includes the completion and emancipation of the human individual,

his deliverance from a superhuman rule and the setting free of the human intellect. The third period, the modern era, means the process of man's transcendence
toward a clearly conceived, objective world of nature and toward a conscious,
organized human community. The theme of this age is the struggle for man's re-
integration in a clearly conceived universe and the struggle for collective order.
(ibid., 21)

17   Cf. Becker's work on the "absolutely serious" (1967, 210-212).

"Lord help me do great things as though they were little since I do them with Your powers; and help me to do little things as though there were great, because I do them in your Name" (Becker 1971, 123).

"He is a thinker; that means,
he knows how to make things
simpler than they are."
(Nietzsche 1974, 205)

CHAPTER 2

LOGOS AS THE AMBIGUITY OF MERGER AND DIVISION

In the beginning of his mature work, Ernest Becker identified the drive for self-esteem as the key motive underlying human action and social organization. But he eventually began to view self-esteem as a symptom of the decay of ancient rituals of worldly rejuvenation, and by the time of his final work, *Escape From Evil*, Becker started to recognize that the motive of guilt-expiation was underneath or perhaps equal to the heroic drive for self-worth. He also began to address the ways that the modern causa sui project attempts to cover-over natural guilt and serves, unfortunately, the pursuit of a one-sided heroics. To Becker's overall sketch, the writings of Kenneth Burke contribute a great deal.

Burke's corpus spans the themes of "motive," "guilt," "ritual," and "ambiguity," and across the lot, he identifies the ambiguous flowerings of logos (speech, language, discourse) as the root source of humanity's natural guilt. But what is meant by "*logos*," and how, specifically, does it bring about (or logically result in) natural guilt? More on this throughout the chapter, but an initial response is that we forever resonate with ambiguous vibrations of merger and division; we are forever caught in tides of symbolic expansion and contraction.[1] Such a depiction offers an overly simple yet remarkably clear definition of what it means to be a person. Thus, where Martin Heidegger characterizes personhood by stating that "the human is a creature of distance!," we tack on the Burkean addendum that distances never sit still. They are subject to endless acts of merger and division, meaning that we exist as ambiguous beings, even in our self-relations. It is because of such ambiguities that humanity naturally walks on the path of natural guilt. We bear natural guilt because we are ineradicably ambiguous and yet we strive for and traffic in what we have taken as "authoritative disambiguation."[2]

In Burke's terms, we construct hierarchies that imply orders of rank and that remain mysterious to each other, and all of this proceeds as we submit to organizing ourselves according to some notion of authority. From this perspective it is easy to see why people so willingly become slavish to institutions and to others; they suffer from logos and accordingly yield to the desire for authoritative disambiguation. Members of highly different social classes can equally yearn for a sanctioning agent or authority that can maintain, at least to varying degrees, some sense of "proper order." But, I must underscore that natural guilt has little to do with being at the top of a hierarchy. Even if we grant that accumulated wealth, social affluence, and material benefits such as those offered by the inheritance structure and property rights are highly relevant and even central to these issues, we should underscore how, in their own terms, they cannot offer the complete story. Natural guilt is the human condition, and we should not reduce the notion of *order* to social-political orders, for it is mainly an ideal order (i.e., some sense of the "natural" order, or a "supernatural" order) that dialectically lends authority to existing social and political states-of-affairs.

To be able to act by way of symbols, which includes the ability to self-consciously choose ends, is to yearn for authority. Is it not obvious that beings who act, beings who are not merely pushed along by the past, encumber the need for legitimate if not authoritative disambiguation? It is the perfect authority, therefore, not merely power, that humans mostly want and need. But if we question where and why authority seems most capable of maintaining itself, we must be ready to fess up: not only do humans remain without metaphysical assurance regarding proper authority, but even their best ideas of perfect order must be carried out in countless less-than-perfect ways. This also implies that authority functions by discounting ambiguities, and hence, beneath all actual, that is "bureaucratized," orders lurks the pangs of conscience that continue to whisper, "arrangements are quite arbitrary and are based upon many factors including happenstance and luck of the draw." Natural guilt, therefore, is a consequence of our always rounding out indeterminacies, of our submitting to various discountings that disambiguate in ways that serve partisan interests.

If some degree of natural guilt is implied by any disambiguation at all, then, in response, people need some kind of redemption, some kind of expiation for their adherence to any given order. On its grim side—and as already shown in the previous chapter—the logic of vicarious substitution enables the fetishization of evil whereby people need not pay up themselves. As the last chapter tried to make evident, people often rally with others around the "song of the scapegoat" and participate in the "cult of the kill." Whereas chapters 4, 5, and 6 will explore some positive strategies and horizons that enable people to expiate guilt within more life-affirming forms of ritual disambiguation, the rest of the present chapter sketches out the basic constitution of logos. I address its operations, structure, and function in discourse, and I try to show that logos, all said, is the root source of natural guilt.

Grounding Logos

In the ancient Stoic worldview, "logos" meant both universal reason as well as the human capacity to reason that distinguishes humanity from other forms of life. Humans are reasonable beings insofar as they bear logos, and so, they have been made in the image of universal reason. Today the term "logos" most likely is associated with advertisements or brand names, but throughout history the word carried diverse meanings including: conversation, argument, measurement, composition, accounting through a story, thought, order, Tao, the clearing that makes room and gathers into a whole.

Logos and the Human Condition

Acknowledging the exceedingly complex sign-systems found throughout the natural kingdom, we find in logos something genuinely radical. Logos, as the human ability to reason, is separated by a gulf from the waggle of bees, the bleating of sheep, the barking of dogs, the signaling of dolphins, or even the signing of apes. The differences here, across the board, are not merely of degree but of kind. Other organisms seem to be enfolded within genetically endowed relevancy structures; various objects and relations are able to ignite interest and enter experience only in accordance with prefigured ranges of relevance. Moreover, animal behavior seems to be an expression of the coordination of genetically prescribed relevancies with whatever is able to enter immediate and proximal sensory awareness. Animals seem fundamentally less concerned with what is transcendent, that is, distant or remote in either space or time.[3] To varying degrees, they are installed concretely in their surrounds, submersively and engrossingly absorbed in ways that humans, existing in the world, are not.[4] Humans are not simply installed in their environments; they are open to the *world,* and therein, natural guilt is an unavoidable consequence of such openness. The phenomenon of "world" must therefore be analytically distinguished from "environment" or "surrounding." We might clarify by saying that plants grow in environments whereas animals live in their surrounds, but only humans, as characterized by logos, exist in the world. To exist in the world is to be sentenced to history.

Logos therefore complicates genetically specified relevancies and makes room for "naturally historical" beings (Anton 2001). Atop and throughout the immediate perceptual flux and flow of the sensory surround, symbolic forms and ritual practices overlay and organize a conceptual order—a living eidos—by which new relevancies may emerge and sustain themselves. Logos, then, is the symptom and the source of our release from the graceful confinements of genetically prefigured relevancies (cf. Herder 1966). Humans surpass overly fixed interests and involvements in their surrounds and have been freed for the purpose of inventing purposes. These rough-cut distinctions, though differently addressed and explained, are similarly argued for by an array of thinkers such as Johann Gottfried Herder,[5] Jakob von Uexküll,[6] Ernst Cassirer,[7] John Dewey,[8] Susanne K. Langer,[9] Adelbert Ames Jr.,[10] Martin Heidegger,[11] Hans Jonas,[12] Walter J. Ong,[13] Marshall McLuhan,[14] and many others. All generally agree upon the importance of carefully attending to the means by which organisms open to what is "around" them.[15] All take seriously the idea that humanity is qualitatively distinct from the rest of the natural world.

The above can be summarized and the below previewed by suggesting that the numerous ways of selectively separating and/or merging always implicate a person who, because of varying levels and points of identification and dis-identification—submissions to different orders, *needing* to say "Yes" or "No" to various prevailing authorities—is thereby guilty. Logos transforms an otherwise submerged transpiring of organismal and vegetative processes into a highly abstract, complex, and agonizingly lived-through drama enacted by personae whose lives play out within bids for cosmic relevance.

Logos as Already Rooted in the Body

If logos is the ground for natural guilt, then where and how is logos grounded? More on this throughout chapter 3, but for present purposes, we begin with the incessant dance of merger and division as it characterizes our bodily existence, noting at least four different horizons of ineradicable ambiguity.[16] I start with the most fundamental, go to the second, third, and final, each time showing finer and finer gradations through which merger and division ebb and flow. This sketch of the bodily basis of logos intends to articulate the meaning of natural guilt and show how natural guilt was forecast by the ambiguities that had to be resolved in the very emergence of the lived-body. Organic and organismal disambiguation, I will further try to show, holds the roots for natural guilt and the individual causa sui project.[17]

First, we know the story of lovers with bodies intertwined, wavering between touching and being touched. Such ambiguous relations can result in a spermatozoon merging with an ovum that then divides within itself and seeks merger with the uterine wall. And how incredibly interesting is the disambiguating merger/division of the placenta and umbilical cord: countless debates hinge upon the precise moment when an individual life starts and/or "removing unwanted tissue" becomes "aborting a baby." And such arrangements are quite temporary, for at the moment of birth, the newborn becomes divided from the mother.[18] Babies become biologically discrete entities, people who are old enough to die; to be alive is already to be among the dying (cf. Lingis 1994).

Life and death are just as much logically related as they are temporally related. This means that even though temporally distinct, life and death are logically one, and this is part of the ambiguity that eternally baffles the living. Mortality, as Hans Jonas suggests, means both that one can die and that one inevitably will die. Not surprisingly, many people, perhaps most, resolve the bulk of the ambiguity by the hopeful fiat that "souls live forever." Unwilling to accept ourselves as ambiguously both living and dying, we wish for life only. We eagerly live in the dream of deathless life, a postmortem life eternal.

Ambiguous lines of merger and division characterize the living body at a second level as well. If you go look at someone, anyone except yourself, you will see a figure against a background. To stand back and look at others is to see discrete bodies who have outlines and so appear to be bound, literally contained, by their fleshy surfaces. Imagine, too, the ways that parents can look directly at their newborns. Now, carefully consider how we see our own bodies. They seem more continuous with the world. Rather than look *to* our own bodies as independent objects out in the world, we look *from* them, and accordingly, entities of the world appear to us only by way of our "focal absence" (cf. Leder 1990). Our bodies are flights of absence, clearings that make room for the very situations in which we find ourselves. Moreover, even though our bodies have visible surfaces and thereby have some sense of being isolated, we are suspended in a wide range of ambiguous contact. We shake hands as well as hold them. We kiss cheeks and put our arms around shoulders. Often enough, we simply want to be near enough that we could touch if the desire would suddenly arise. Try to imagine spending the rest of your life without ever being touched again by another person. Such a life would be unbearable.

In the modern world, and in significant contrast to traditional societies, our lives are highly indebted to others whom we personally have never come into contact with and whom we never will. The consequence is that we now pretend that our personhood is independent of any particular others. But that is the lie. Contemplate for a moment how dependent we are upon other people, especially distant unknown others. In almost every way, the practices we enjoy, foods we eat, music we listen to, clothes we wear, roads we drive on, all of these were made possible by anonymous others. It is the sheer functionality of anonymity that enables us to eagerly and proudly overestimate our sense of separateness and autonomy.[19]

Aligning with life over death and assuming independence from others, we also commonly cover-over the many ambiguous mergers and divisions embodied in eating and defecating. Food eternally remains a gift in the fullest and most profound sense of the word. It is so thoroughly a gift that it easily embarrasses the modern secular humanist. Indeed,

> If at the end of each person's life he were to be presented with the living spectacle of all that he had organismically incorporated in order to stay alive, he might well feel horrified by the living energy he had ingested…the average person, would be taken up with hundreds of chickens, flocks of lambs and sheep, a small herd of steers, sties full of pigs, and rivers of fish. The din alone would be deafening. (Becker 1975, 2)

So much must be sacrificed if we are to continue living. Should we be surprised at the history of table manners and dinnertime prayers? Do we not owe at least some reverence to what has been sacrificed for our continuance? And what of the other side of this issue: the way that we try not to dwell too long on the immense waste we produce and the footprint we leave behind. It boggles the mind to think of every way that our continuance produces both material and biological waste. And what must be identified here is not merely all the food we eat and the mess we leave behind, but all that we consume including the infrastructure involved in producing what becomes refuse in our wake.

We try to not think of how our lives are implicated in the deprivations of others and are consuming limited resources. But the unseemly truth is that we live by feeding upon life. Vampires fascinate us perhaps because they are mythic images representing a repressed recognition of the alien other within. They stand for our wide-awake unwillingness to admit that we continue by consuming vital fluids of the living.

The fourth embodied dance of merger and division is perhaps the most elusive of all. For it can be considered only when we are awake. The fact is, though, that we all spend a good part of our lives in the vegetative state of dreamless sleep (cf. Anton 2006), and we are naturally guilty of covering this over. We seem unwilling to admit: that awakeness is only part of the whole of human life, or that awakeness is always already less than the whole of our being, or that all of our wide-awake concerns are but a part of who we are, or that all of us are the same while we dreamlessly sleep. What would the world be like if all persons everywhere fully grasped that each and every day we all recede from all worldly cares?

We are earthly and vegetative beings—anything but the fully autonomous and independent beings we takes ourselves to be in awakeness—and this, precisely, is the ambiguous truth from which we routinely try to hide. Dreamless sleep reveals how needy we are. It so thoroughly humbles and discloses vulnerability that any presumption to full self-sufficiency is openly discredited, revealed as a false pretense. We so thoroughly fill our eyes with symbols of self-sufficiency that, at all costs, we try to hide our utter dependency upon a mysterious whole from which we only on occasion are released.

And so goes the self-sufficiency parade: We pretend that humans do not really die. We act as if people are who they are independently of others. We hide from the fact that people are the food they eat and the refuse they leave behind. We reduce the whole of life to the activities and concerns of awake existence. All of these taken together, as illustrations of our assent to suspect disambiguations, are inseparable from the modern causa sui project. Across the lot, we conceal the facts of finitude and dependence at every opportunity. But the lived-body itself is thoroughly characterized by the ebb and flow of merger and division, and it should not be surprising that logos perfects itself by growing and developing in the soil of its origin. As quivering and palpating beings who were born and inevitably will die, who consume the material world and spew waste in the wake, and who are vegetative for a fair portion of our lives, we are not who we commonly believe we are. Our disambiguations hold so many repressed ambiguities. We are much older, larger, and other than we normally presume, and therein lies the bodily ground of logos and of natural guilt.

Requisite Operations of Discourse

The basic and recurrent operations of all discourse are merger and division. These operations are typified in acts of definition, and in particular, in the use of the categories "genus" and "species." Even more generally stated, "all languages must have words that put things together and words that take things apart" (Burke 1961, 297). Throughout history and across cultures we find an awesome range regarding what has been brought together (i.e., regarded in terms of "continuity") and what has been taken apart (i.e., regarded in terms of "discontinuity").

Discursive Merger and Division

Losing the innocence of graceful installment within the immediate surround, humans come to flash in and out of transparent submersion. At points we can feel estranged from world in ways unknown to other creatures, while at other points we can feel the satisfaction of a union or contact with nature in ways that seem denied to other animals. As Burke says:

> Any such medium will be, as you prefer, either a way of "dividing" us from
> the "immediate" (thereby setting up a kind of "alienation" at the very start
> of our emergence from infancy to that state of articulacy somewhat mislead-

ingly called the "age of reason"); or it can be viewed as a paradoxical way of "uniting" us with things on a "higher level of awareness," or some such. (Here again, we encounter our principles of continuity and discontinuity). (1966, 52)

Logos estranges us from the immediate surround but in doing so puts us in possession of a possible reuniting with nature on a higher realm of contact.[20] We can encounter the world as it can be known in terms of its essences, its eternal forms, its mathematical regularities.[21] We are partly unlike any other animal because we can behold with awe the pervasive sense of order and design throughout the cosmos.

Merger and division operate at a second level as well. Others become separate from us but we therein gain the capacity to commune with them in deeper and more profound ways. Logos is the condition by which we can be at a great distance from others, radically disconnected and disidentified, but it also enables us to encounter others in their interiority and to grow intimate with them. With words people can create a "we" and an "us," but they also can create a "them" or an "it." Nationalisms and other forms of tribal identification have been made possible because people identify with those who speak the same language and disidentify with those who speak an alien tongue. This means that any and every language, and *every speech act too*, is both inclusionary *and* exclusionary on a variety of levels. People not only commence and sustain various kinds of relationships with words, they often use words to end them. In short, discourse divides individuals from others as much as it merges people together (cf. Crable 2009).

The basic operations of discursive merger and division bear upon even the solitary individual, for persons become both estranged from and reunited with themselves. Divided within ourselves, as if once removed, we gain a sense of self-awareness through inner dialogue, and there are always ineradicable splits between the self who speaks, the self who listens, and the self who is spoken about.[22] We remain one step away from ourselves; we never enjoy pure and full access. There is, as Josiah Royce suggests, "no royal road to self-knowledge," and so, having a self, at all, is a kind of estrangement, an ongoing event of disambiguation that holds changing scopes of significance.

The merger and division operating within discourse are also displayed in the temporal sensibilities by which people unite and/or separate "past," "present," and "future." By use of grammatical tenses, dimensions of past, present, and future can seem either separate or continuous. Merging together future, present, and past, we disclose human lives as wholes or as part of many generations. But divisions also can temporalize temporality in ways that isolate the moment of now. Here time, as a present moment, seems to drag on and on. The past is tenuously connected and fading, and likewise, future events of varying timescale can vibrate between assured and unreachable. At one moment, people may grope unsuccessfully for meaningful connections between the discrete events comprising their lives, while at other moments, the whole seems definite and in order. In general, shifting lines of merger and division—identifications and disidentifications both having varying scope—keep humans in an ambiguously awkward relationship to time.

In different ways, these four examples of merger and division help to sketch the human as variously expansive, variously constrictive, and discursively merging and dividing all along. As expansive, we are able to identify with more than the boundaries of the skin. We can become identified with (or "consubstantial with") the whole of existence; we can recognize that we, each and every one of us, are places and moments of all that ever will exist. At other times we can feel insignificant, irrelevant, not in any way meaningfully connected to the whole of existence. As expansive, we can look to our navels and see the permanent mark of sociality, the proof of our deep connectedness. As divisive, we can look to the skin and see ourselves as cut-off and separated from others, profoundly alone. We can feel the connectedness of love and friendship but we also can feel the isolation of indifference and abandonment. Natural guilt, I have been trying to make abundantly clear, emerges from the always-unsettled boundaries that separate us and bring us together; it comes from being set adrift (or perhaps swimming) in the forever changing tides of division and merger.

Despite our incessant attempts at authoritative disambiguation, ambiguity is ineradicable; we cannot, with one summative and eternal word, say all of our different mergers and divisions. In any attempt to say any of them, we must begin somewhere. And, one relation must come prior while another comes later; one must take the lead while another gets the last word. Consider the pair "merger and division" and then "division and merger," or how about the pair "good and evil" compared to "evil and good." Each pair has a feel about it, and that feel emerges from the relative position of each term in the pair. Depending upon which term we begin with and which term we end with—even when there are only two terms—we find a nascent narrative, a mini drama.[23]

Symbolic Action, Concepts, and "God" Terms

Burke's master trilogy, (Grammar, Rhetoric, and Symbolic) loosely corresponds to the pentad, the guilt-cycle, and to the many means of symbolic expiation. These three areas characterize, in a rough and broad sketch, the main differences between scientific language, rhetorical language, and poetic language, respectively.[24] Science is used mainly in preparation for action, rhetoric is used to induce action or attitude (with attitude being an act-in-the-making), and art is a form of action in its own right in and for itself.[25] But caution needs to be exercised in these delineations, for language is never merely a means to action, as if our words could be exclusively a preparation for action. All speech is a kind of action in its own regard: it is symbolic action.

Logos, therefore, is suasive even in denotative propositions, and likewise, "spontaneous speech is not a naming at all," argues Burke, "but a system of attitudes, of implicit exhortations. To call a man a friend or enemy is *per se* to suggest a program of action with regard to him" (1954, 177). To name and thereby identify a substance is to imply motives for action, and likewise, motives for action assume some substance identified or at the least nameable (cf. Kenny 2000). The world's many different nomenclatures and vernaculars, argues Burke in his "Terministic Screens," operate by different principles of continuity and discontinuity; they reflect reality by a selection that is also a deflection, and so, each terminology tracks down different motivations and ends. As Burke states in *A Grammar of Motives*, "one's initial act in choosing 'where to draw the line' by choosing terms that merge or terms that divide has an anticipatory effect upon one's conclusions" (1962, 415). Still, the dialectical point is that just as the suasive and hortatory is nestled within even the most scientific of discourse, so too there is a unique and peculiar kind of insight within even the most poetic forms of speech. Logos enables us to talk about aspects of the world.[26]

Susanne K. Langer's chapter "Language," from her *Philosophy in a New Key* is highly instructive in this regard. She maintains that "the transformation of experience into concepts, not the elaboration of signals and symptoms, is the motive of language" (1942, 103). Her point is that the primary functions of speech are to create concepts and then to wean those concepts from their original installment. Discourse mints concepts and then releases them from their local, original, and accidental contexts, and so lends conscious command over an infinitely expanding horizon of interaction. "Denotation is the essence of language," Langer writes,

> because it frees the symbol from its original instinctive utterance and marks its deliberate *use*, outside of the total situation that gave it birth. A denotative word…weans the conception away from the purely momentary and personal experience and fastens it on a permanent element which may enter into all sorts of situations. (1942, 108)

Concepts, Langer maintains, are first released from their total and actual situation by denotative speech, and furthermore, it is also by such speech that we gain conscious command over our concepts (cf. Taylor 1995). Decontextualizable and under conscious direction, concepts are freed from installment in the perceptual surround and become open for employment in a variety of settings.

The above can be explained more fully by examining one of the peculiar properties of speech: analytic predication. What is inseparably infused (i.e., what is both/and) at the level of perception comes to be divided conceptually. Of the immediate sensory surround, logos divides and isolates, and then, in a bringing-back-together, it articulates various relations that it had first separated. Logos thus tears asunder and then builds-together in such a way that various relations can be disambiguated. As Erwin Straus observes,

> Freshmen in high school Latin are given the practice sentence, "The table is round." Notwithstanding its simplicity, something is accomplished in this sentence which cannot be equaled by any physical force, no matter how great: the divorcing of the "roundness" from the table. (1966, 184)

The table can be separated from its roundness. The top half can be spoken of as if it were independent of the bottom half. The table can be thought of as independent of its color. Analytic predication is thus that power of merger and division that enables us to think: "that cup is round," or "that sound is quiet," or "this ink is black." In each of these simple cases, logos separates what remains inseparable at the level of sensory or perceptual experience. Indeed, people can say that a person is sleeping, or that a person is eating, or even that a person is doing nothing.[27] The mergers and divisions of logos, said simply, make room for things and actions, as if both actions and things could be independent of their concrete occurrence within the whole of non-repeatable, non-decontextualizable existence.[28]

Concepts are not only freed from the flux of perceptual immediacy, they move toward greater and greater abstraction, so great in fact that they now resemble titles. To help clarify how abstract concepts in language can drift far from any perceptual particular, Burke offers the notion of "entitlement." He writes,

> Thus with the sentence, "The man walks down the street": To realize that it is more like the 'title' of a situation than like the description of the act, we need but realize that the sentence, as stated, could not be illustrated. For you'd have to picture a tall man, or a short man, a dark man or a light man, etc. He'd have to be pictured as walking upright or bent over, with or without a hat, or a cane, etc. And the street would have to be wide or narrow, with a certain kind of curbing, paving, and the like. (1966, 361)

Freed from installment within any particular situation, concepts become finer and finer distillations. Operating by way of synecdoche and metonymy, logos omits more and more, and this means that essences, or "Platonic forms," and what Burke calls "god-terms," are not in some other-than-empirical realm, nor are they locked inside an individual's mind. They naturally arise by way of merger across time accompanied by divisions in space. We compare instances, or glean from cases across time, in ways that simultaneously discount differences. To look at five sculptures and find each beautiful in its own way is to do precisely this, and likewise, to look at a cat and then a dog and then to call them both "animals" is to do this as well. All embracing god-terms, therefore, are the consequence and the natural end product of the mergers and divisions of logos: by the art of omission, essential parts are allowed a more articulated definition.

Humans have a taste for the eternal only because of the many essences that logos makes possible. Words themselves give direct experience of transcendence and so they lend intelligibility to our sense of the timeless. In the "Epilogue: Prologue in Heaven," from *The Rhetoric of Religion*, Burke has The Lord (TL) say to Satan (S):

> By the tests of sheer animality, the "deathless essences" of sheer symbolic-ity will be a mockery. Yet, by their own tests, they really will transcend the sheerly material realm of corruption and death. The fall of all the trees in the world will not bring down the meaning of the word "tree." By the sheer act of utterance as such, there is a sense in which time will be transcended...In this sense the speech that teaches them to despair will be able, by its sheer nature as definition, to be as though enduring...In this technical sense, meanings re-ally do transcend time. Yet once you have said as much, the fact remains that, once the beings who understand a given language cease to be, the sweetest poem written in those words is dead. (1961, 305-306)

Humans can speak of "love everlasting" or "timeless truths," or even of "the eter-nal," but they may recognize how short, discrete, and quickly ending are all such terms. And yet people do take themselves seriously when they speak of things such as: "all" and "everything," or "forever." Indeed, how can they not? Imagine two young adults, holding hands and looking into each other's eyes as they pro-nounce: "I'll love you forever." Or consider this: someone sitting all alone in a dark room, face buried within tear-soaked palms, thinks: "Things will never get any better." Who does not know of experiences such as these? For the people who are currently dwelling in such expansions or contractions, some kind of horizon of transcendence is being experienced. And this is genuine transcendence, not merely illusion or artifice. Such transcendence is also made evident in the ability to make promises, for promises allow an expansion, a reaching beyond oneself. In a word, "To say that man is a symbol-using animal is by the same token to say that he is a *transcending* animal" (Burke 1962, 716). Logos, as a source of transcendence, gives humans their first real taste of timelessness. It is the fruit by which we are seduced to imagine that aspects of life—including ourselves—are not subject to becoming and change. We may become so seduced by symbols that we now desire everything, including the desire to live forever. But once again, restless ambiguities abound: we cannot have everything, nor can we live forever. And, no unambiguous order can be spoken in a world that permanently refuses to sit still.

I have been somewhat round-aboutly probing the grounds of natural guilt by explicating the basic operations of logos. I now more explicitly address how the drive toward "god-terms" such as "reason," "God's will," "law," or the "nature of things" dialectically relates to the sociopolitical order, and therein, I address how logos intertwines with natural guilt and the possibilities of guilt expiation. By moving from the *operations* of discourse to its *structure* and *function*, I accordingly turn attention away from how logos operates and toward what we end up doing to ourselves and others by way of it.

Structure and Function of Discourse

Logos bears directly upon motivation and social order, and this can be clarified if we focus upon the *structure* and *function* of discourse.[29] The *structure* of any spoken account of human motives will need to disambiguate along the lines and ratios of "act," "agent," "scene," "agency," and "purpose." Burke's well-known and highly used "pentad" thus refers to the necessary structure involved in any account of motives. The *function* of our talk about motives, on the other hand, is to disambiguate in accordance with the yearning for authoritative order and to manage relations implied therein. Plainly stated, people desire order, make promises, and accept vows (all of which are ways of saying, "I will not do P, and I will do Q"), and so people always place themselves on the "tautological cycle of terms": guilt, hierarchy, redemption, victimage.

Structure

First and foremost, the substances of both the pentad and the guilt-cycle are highly paradoxical, ineradicably fraught with ambiguity. In the introduction to *A Grammar of Motives* Burke suggests that pentadic motivations are assigned and disputed—verbally "placed" and thus disambiguated—only because of ambiguity. "There must remain," Burke writes,

> something essentially enigmatic about the problem of motives, and that this underlying enigma will manifest itself in inevitable ambiguities and inconsistencies among the terms for motives. Accordingly, what we want is not terms that avoid the ambiguity, but terms that clearly reveal the strategic spots at which ambiguities necessarily arise...instead of considering it our task to "dispose of" any ambiguity, we rather consider it our task to study

and clarify the resources of ambiguity…it is in the areas of ambiguity that
transformations take place. (1962, xx-xxi)

To illustrate these ideas, let me offer a range of cases, each moving along pentadic lines, where ambiguity allows for disambiguation but implies a guilt-ridden repression or deflection of other possibilities. (Addressed from the happier side, any disambiguation holds nascent resources for its own transformation). Consider, for starters, the disambiguation involved in scenic placements. All acts whatsoever must receive placement within a circumference that is neither the only nor the necessary one. People directly confront their own freedom as they recognize their ability to delimit any "act" within different scopes or circumferences. For example, I am just as equally a place and moment of the universe as I am an animal in an environment as I am a person from a lineage.[30] As Burke suggests, "For instance, I am writing these words 'in Florida this January,' or during a lull in the bombing of North Vietnam,' or 'in a period following the invention of the atomic bomb but prior to a soft landing of electronic instruments on the surface of the moon,' and so on" (1966, 360). Ultimately, to select a circumference, Burke writes, "is in itself an act, an 'act of faith'" (1962, 84). The endlessly ongoing expansive and constrictive flow of logos furthermore means that people are "continually performing 'new acts' in that they are continually making judgments as to the scope of the context which they implicitly or explicitly impute to their interpretation of motives" (1962, 90).[31]

Disambiguations holding repressed ambiguities are also illustrated in the use of age to permit or deny authority regarding various acts. Think about the applicability of drinking laws, sex laws, gambling laws, and varieties of legal sanctions, all in accordance with someone's age. Hugh Dalziel Duncan writes, "The status incongruities in our relationship with adolescents we think old enough to send off into the army, yet too young to remain on the streets after ten o'clock, are equally embarrassing" (1962, 307). Age, a mark of an agent which is mostly scenic, serves to authoritatively disambiguate, and so, we act as if being eighteen or twenty-one years old means something all by itself. From all of the facts that could be made relevant to any particular action or decision, how arbitrary seems this focus on age? Moreover, how many other motives gain their impetus by basically capitalizing on and exploiting such arbitrary disambiguation? For example, without having to assess personal history, employment records—*anything other than age*—credit card companies can apply loan shark rates to money lent to young adults.

Tiny changes, such as alterations of a conjunctive word or two, can alter everything. Clearest case: "Shifts of interpretation result," Burke suggests, "from the different ways in which we group events in the *because of, in spite of,* and *re-*

gardless of categories" (1954, 36). Indeed, how many debates roll and tumble by selections therein? How much persuasive speech (i.e., rhetoric) moves implicitly or explicitly by positioning along those categories? How many stories open to other possibilities by looking for a transformation precisely in these terms? At the end of the day, this means that "Metaphysics might be described as an attempt to decide which proposition we should connect with a 'therefore,' which we should connect with a 'however,' and which with a sheer 'and'" (Burke 1962, 406).

Function

In response to the unending ambiguities of logos, each and every person is guilty of trying to resolve them or disambiguate them by aligning with various orders. We are, as Burke suggests, goaded by the spirit of hierarchy, meaning that the "guilt-cycle" characterizes the basic function of all motivational discourse. In his commentary upon "Human Behavior Considered Dramatistically," Burke (1954) writes, "the attempt here is to consider what should be the over-all terms for naming relationships and developments that, *mutatis mutandia*, are likely to figure in all human association. To that end, the stress is placed upon the motives of Guilt, Redemption, Hierarchy, and Victimage that supplement and modify men's purely natural or biological inclinations" (274). These terms are likely to figure in all human association for three main reasons. First, each and every individual must say "Yes" or "No" to various sociopolitical orders. It is in this demand for an attitude of either acceptance or rejection that history necessarily repeats itself.[32] The "eternally recurring same" of human life is the existential fact of each individual facing already existing social orders, having to either grant or deny their authority. Second, to be able to say "Yes" to a vow or promise is to open to the future in such a way that one also needs to say "No" to an immediate self, which further reveals how "temptation is but a tautological aspect of the idea of 'Order'" (1961, 194). The very meaning of the term "promise" implies a creature who is open to failure. Were we not given the possibility of failure, we could neither give nor receive a promise or vow. In this sense guilt is tautological with the freedom to make promises. Third, our action is divided into various roles and these often have conflicting values and make conflicting demands. Often people are conflicted even within themselves; part of the struggle to disambiguate refers to what Duncan calls the development of "inner audiences." And so, the perennial struggle is to help people cooperate and live at peace with themselves regardless of having said "Yes" to different orders.[33] Burke nicely summarizes these points where he writes: "There is implicit in reason the need for 'justification' (which is *per se* the evidence of guilt)…Accordingly, we hold that one cannot 'debunk' guilt completely without arriving at a disintegrative, anti-social philosophy…

Freedom from guilt would be freedom from public reference, from sociality" (1984, 164-165).

A major implication is that rhetoric, suasive discourse, is easily misunderstood if it is cast as little more than individuals in acts of compliance gaining. On the contrary, persuasive discourse is best grasped by first attending to the larger orders that are submitted to before individual persons begin their rhetorical appeals. This is how self-persuasion accompanies rhetoric. People often fortify and confirm their adherence to an order by gaining cohorts. Person A, therefore, is consubstantial with person B in regard to order X. Identification and consubstantiality, by the paradoxes of substance, move us well beyond one person aligning to another. We can identify with others' causes, their interests, and take their gods as our own. On its grimmer side, we can be misled by cunning and treachery, serve others' gods as if they were our own, all only to realize that we have been betrayed.

We want comrades, fellow members of the "proper" order to be served. Part of this drive comes because we are dialogic creatures, and we naturally incline toward an authoritative dialogic partner to address, someone with whom we can plead our cases, someone with whom we check our values and gain perspective upon ourselves. God, nature, science, love, money, family, friendship, tradition, the state, law, these are the main organizing principles that most people use to give authoritative shape and pattern (i.e., motive) to their decisions and actions. Persuasion, especially when grasped in terms of identification and consubstantiality, always implies some sense of order. It is by order that we act.

Ambiguities, Guilt, and Order

We must be able to celebrate ambiguity if we are to learn from Burke's writings. Almost all of his key concepts, ideas, and arguments are made possible because he carefully chooses words that have ambiguously overpopulated meanings. Consider the many ambiguities that he identifies between logical relations and temporal relations. Even the word "first," for example, slips back and forth between two kinds of priority, the logically prior and the temporally prior. Other examples include: his *four master tropes* ("metaphor," "metonymy," "synecdoche," and "irony"): "Give a man but one of them, tell him to exploit its possibilities, and if he is thorough in doing so, he will come upon the other three" (1962, 503-517); *identification*: "…put identification and division ambiguously together, so that you cannot know for certain just where one ends and the other begins, and you have the characteristic invitation to rhetoric" (1962, 549); *dialectical substance*: "Here again we confront the ambiguities of substance, since symbolic communication is not a merely external instrument, but also intrinsic to men as agents. Its motivational properties characterize both 'the human situation' and what men are 'in themselves'" (1962, 33); *paradox of purity or paradox of the absolute*: "the paradox of the absolute figures grammatically in the dialectic, making for a transcending of one term by its other, and for the reversed ambiguous derivation of the term from its other as ancestral principle" (1962, 38); *symbolism as condensation and displacement*: "Substitution sets the conditions for 'transcendence,'… The subterfuges of euphemism can carry this process still further, culminating in the resources of idealization that Plato perfected through his dialectic of Upward Way and Downward Way" (1966, 8); *perfection*: "the principle of drama is implicit in the idea of action, and the principle of victimage is implicit in the nature of drama…Inasmuch as substitution is a prime resource of symbol systems, the conditions are set for catharsis by scapegoat" (1966, 18); *perspective by incongruity*: "the placing of special stress upon the kinds of hermeticism, or stylistic mercureality, that are got by the merging of categories once felt to be mutually exclusive" (1954, 69). As all these different quotations illustrate, each taken from some of Burke's key writings, it is by the very resources of ambiguity that the many transformations proceed.

A further case in point, one calling for even more detailed treatment, is the way Burke uses the word "order." Because the word "order" nests so many meanings, it well serves those who would study the rhetorical underbelly of discourse. For one thing, "order," in Burke's terms, is not a "positive term," but a kind of "fiction" (cf. 1961, 180-183). It is a "dialectical substance," a "polar word" whose sense is partly defined by not being its opposite. The term "order" therefore takes its meaning, in part, by being the contrast to terms such as "disorder," "disarray," or simply "a mess." Order is an arrangement that has things set in their proper place, and the notion of "proper" relies upon some kind of authority. Similarly, there is the expression "order of arrangement," which implies a series of steps where one step has to be done before another (as in the "order of operations" in solving math equations). Order thus implies priority and a kind of privileging of firsts. But it also aligns to ends, as in doing something "in order to" have something else happen. On a wholly different front, the term "order" connotes a sect or small grouping, as when a profession, occupation, or cause creates a body known as an order. Yet even within these orders, "order" commonly (and quite ambiguously) means rank and so implies the hierarchies of social stratification. People speak of social order or even of social inequalities as part of the "natural order." Interestingly, "order," used as a verb, is often synonymous with the word command, as in "Someone in the military ordering someone to carry out a mission." But even here, a further ambiguity crops up: orders can be commands as well as kinds of requests. For example, a manager can order an employee to do an unseemly task while a customer can order up a couple drinks. In both cases, those who make the orders also provide the larger order that mainly motivates the action: money.

The Negative Order of Property Rights

My concluding examination of suspect diamabiguations, that is, disambiguations holding repressed ambiguities, focuses upon private property and property rights. By means of logos people merge themselves with their property while dividing others from it. The order enabled therein comes by way of the negative. Such negativity first appears as the "hortatory don't" as in "Don't touch; this is mine, meaning *not* yours." "Mine and thine," as Burke suggests, brim with the "secret sacred sign of negativity": "No Trespassing." This means that we today are alienated and homeless, no longer free to graze upon the natural fruits of the earth. In the modern United States many people not only own the land that they live upon, they can "own" distant lands, even inherit property that they have never visited. We must ask, therefore, in accordance to what authority are these possessions and property rights justified?[34]

Although the owning of property is authorized both in the Bible and in the U.S. Constitution, the lines demarcating ownership or possession are invisible, ambiguous, and often need to be maintained by some kind of physical authority. First it was barbarically by conquest and occupancy, then by Imperial command and outpost, then by Kingly, Lordly, and religious "right," and finally by political institutions that rely upon federal, state, and local legal apparatus. These historical developments, I should stress, took shape and gained their momentum before anybody had a full awareness of what was happening, and people have come to clear self-awareness about such things only after they become personally involved and complicit. This is partly why people find it a bitter pill to accept the idea that private property is the mark of the "Satanic." In sum, then,

> Things that in themselves are positive, but...in becoming labeled "mine" and "thine," take on the secret sacred sign of negativity....The negative, as so ingrained through the subtleties of "conscience," will build up a sense of guilt equally as vast and complicated as this bundle of negatively protected properties. And from this sense of guilt there will arise the yearning for a new and all-inclusive positive, the demand for a supernal sacrifice literally existing and somehow serving by his suffering both to cancel off this guilt and to sanction the perpetuating of the conditions out of which the guilt arises. (Burke 1961, 285)

The argument here, if it is not yet explicit enough, is that the pervasive Christian notion that "Christ is the way of salvation" basically makes sense to people whose sense of guilt is so pent up that they now believe that only a supernatural sacrifice could correct the wrongdoings.

People in the modern Western world, and the U.S. in particular, have accepted the "negative" orders of private property, usury, inheritance, and increasingly the privatization of commons. How much guilt comes from these suspect disambiguations? How deeply must some people sense that private ownership is an arbitrary disambiguation backed by a dubious authority? How much rapaciousness toward the world and others is possible for the possessive individual? How much victimage occurs to redeem such internal divisiveness? This line of questioning is framed even more pointedly where Burke writes:

> Insofar as all complex social order will necessarily be grounded in some kind of property structure, and insofar as all such order in its divisive aspects makes for the kind of social malaise which theologians would explain in terms of "original sin," is it possible that rituals of victimage are the "natural" means for affirming the principle of social cohesion above the principle of social division? (1954 286)

Repressed guilt, a symptom of the alignment with institutions of private property and private ownership (even "paid for" disambiguations such as "already owned land") is a major source of violence and social evil. There are countless fronts of inward social injustice and countless fronts of outward violence upon "alien-other" scapegoats. So much sickness of spirit comes from a conscience that feels the guilt of having said "Yes" to property rights and inheritance laws, of having said "Yes" to authorities that serve partisan interests. Seriously, if you personally did nothing particularly wrong but benefited greatly from the wrongdoings of others, are you not at least complicitous? Who in the modern Western world could escape complicity in this level of guilt? You may want to be on the lookout for the backlash of a denied guilty-conscience: you may be the next scapegoat. We, too, need to become more reflectively aware of our own drives toward scapegoating.[35]

The conclusion to be drawn from this discussion is not that we should all give up our property, join hands, and sing beautiful songs together. We simply need to recognize that ownership and property rights are saturated in negativity, fundamentally ambiguous, morally questionable, and "naturally" generative of guilt. We must learn how to recognize this guilt, to minimize it, and manage it. For starters, it is one thing to sit, watch, and defend one's current staying spot.[36] It is quite another to own distant property and legally retain it unused or unoccupied. It is a wholly other thing to bestow it by inheritance laws. The task, then, is not necessarily to give up property; one need not go the way of the communist or the ascetic hermit.[37] Minimally, we need to recognize and accept that ownership and wealth accumulation are fundamentally ambiguous and will naturally generate guilt.

Fortunately, not all sacrificial redemption need vent upon a scapegoat. There are ample resources for heroic expiation, for example, to be found in acts of mortification. This means that victimage and sacrifice have three main forms: homicidal sacrifice, suicidal sacrifice, and ritual mortification. Homicidal sacrifice is cheap and rapacious, ever partly unsatisfied because its logic keeps life and death separate. One person kills so that others may prosper. In suicidal sacrifice, people willingly kill themselves, and others too, in their efforts to serve a holy cause or mission. In ritual mortification, people civilly attempt to bring beauty to the world, even to the point of allowing others to harm them or put them to death. Socrates and Jesus are commonly offered as exemplar cases. Mortification, *living a dying life*, is the most powerful resource for heroic guilt expiation. It is, as Burke argues, the "subtlest term of all" (1961, 190). Accordingly, I devote chapters 4, 5, and 6 to different lines of neo-Stoic heroism, each of which explores finer possibilities of ritual mortification.[38] At present I only suggest that the kinds of disambiguations to be sought are not those that err toward the side of removing agency, but neither do they fall toward the modern causi sui project.

Summary and Transition

Everything born will one day die, and so the living must fight for survival. But the story of humanity is often a tale of the drive for a kind of survival after death. If we were to ask Ernest Becker, "From where comes such yearnings?," he likely would have offered something similar to the following response: humans are animals but by the ingenuity of symbolic designations they have been able to self-reflexively grasp their own death. Human symbolicity, the ability to say "I," with all of its corresponding identifications and implications, precipitates into the flight of heroic death denial. At first pass this might seem highly similar to Kenneth Burke's claim that we are "bodies who learn language" and we are "rotten with perfection." But crucial differences must not be overlooked.

Burke's understanding of language unavoidably hinges upon a comparative notion of divine action, or, at the least, a notion of "final cause" that was long ago abandoned by the modern scientific world-picture that Becker often relies upon. Moreover, from a Burkean perspective, Becker partly undercuts the possibilities of living myth by his tragic posture of psychoanalytic debunking.[39] Said otherwise, Becker's naturalist slant sometimes advances by casting a super-imaginary notion of transcendence to which he then comparatively depicts symbols and language as a kind of cheap stucco. Look carefully at the introduction to *Escape from Evil*, for example, where Becker writes, "...there is really no basic distinction between sacred and profane in the symbolic affairs of men. As soon as you have symbols you have artificial self-transcendence via culture" (1975, 4). In one sense, Becker is saying that symbols inevitably challenge the dichotomy between sacred and profane, but in the same breath he suggests that the sacred is actually "artificial."[40] The dichotomy is indeed collapsed, but unwittingly toward the profane as he, in Burke's terms, "translates in a downward way." Becker's commitment to a scientific naturalism and biological individualism somewhat over determines his text to conclude that symbols are but "a figment of the imagination for flesh-and-blood organisms" (ibid.). Theology is therefore necessary illusion, creative fiction that people need for psychological reasons. Starting with humans as animals, Becker may have unwittingly truncated the meaning of symbol-using.

For Becker, ambiguity refers mainly to the existential dread of being both animal and spirit. For Burke, ambiguity is more thoroughgoing and far more reaching. Only ambiguous beings can act; ambiguity is the forcing bed of genuine transcendence. As always already depending upon the act of defining circumference, one is arguably not even a body, but an ecstatic place and moment (cf. Anton 2001. As Burke puts it: "Whenever we find a distinction between the internal and the external, the intrinsic and the extrinsic, the within and the without, (as with Korzybski's distinction between happenings 'inside the skin' and happenings 'outside the skin') we can expect to encounter the paradoxes of substance" (1962, 47). If only by contrast to Becker, Burke's position is a bit more resistant to zoological and/or ethological frames regarding personhood and motives for action.

By the terms of Burke's "secular conversions," Becker's vocabulary begins in upward conversion only to spiral tragically by conversion downward. His account thus underestimates how logos is the source of many ways of transcending the conditions of animality. Transcendence does not merely open us to recognizing our limits; it opens us to identifications with the cosmos that are profoundly wider than other animals can experience. We actually transcend our bodily surfaces by the use of symbols and therein experience the possibility of living transpersonally, even eternally.

But beings who can overstep their boundaries are forever guilty beings. In expansively commending ourselves and presumptively garnering a position of self-sufficiency, guilt emerges. And it emerges, too, from denying our individuation, denying the calls made upon us because of our uniqueness. The difficulty is that we are forever unsure of claiming too much or too little for ourselves; we, as humans, suffer the guilt of living through the eternally protean lines of merger and division. In one instant, we can take on expansiveness, feel as if our lives genuinely mean something and make a difference; at other times, we can see ourselves as little other than "complex and fancy worm food."[41] Ambiguously related to the whole of the cosmos and awkwardly placed in existence, humans remain perennially guilty, for there are always new needs for further disambiguation. So where does this leave us?

Burke concludes the "Ends and Means" of his *A Grammar of Motives* with a suggestion that the constant contemplation of human foibles could serve "Towards the Purification of War."[42] He suggests that we laugh at how we create trouble for ourselves in our yearning for an all-authoritative order and in our denial of all authority. He says that we should neither fall into the cult of proselytizing absolutes nor fall into self-serving indifference. Instead, Burke writes, "we must turn precisely in the direction of a neo-Stoic cosmopolitanism, with ideals of tolerance and resignation to the bureaucratic requirements implicit in the structure of modern industry and commerce. The only alternatives are fanaticism and dissipation" (1962, 318). By "fanaticism" Burke implies the mania of the one, a yearning for absolute authority in one's disambiguation, the imposition of one terminology of motives. By the notion of "dissipation," Burke implies the delirium of the many, a kind of helpless, low-visioned, self-serving rapaciousness that grabs and gulps whatever is nearest to hand. If dissipation easily results from debunkers who too skeptically conclude that that "everything is too ambiguous and so I am just looking out for myself," fanaticism results from those who are seduced to reduce all of life to religious order, scientific order, military order, or the state.

The position that Burke calls for, one that falls between fanaticism and dissipation, was already touched upon in Becker's claim that one's "character armor" becomes a prison if individuals unnecessarily limit their life practices. We need to meditate upon the complexity of human motives, upon the many ways that one-dimensional heroics fail, especially when those heroics boil down to nothing more than money-handling (investing, owning, and other "non-creative" employments with capital). The uniquely human modes of transcendence are possible wherever one actually, genuinely, tries to transform something, struggles to create something, attempts make or build or articulate something. Where and when people struggle to the best of their wills to create a poem, a dance, a small wooden ship, they achieve transcendence and transform both themselves and the world, all by nothing more than their authentic effort.

The whole of Part II offers a neo-Stoic heroism, one that explores the possibilities of ritual mortification and worldly rejuvenation. But before moving on to the second part of this book, I need to conclude Part I by tracing logos as well as natural guilt back to their cosmological grounds. This study began with the contemporary drive of self-esteem, moved to an account of natural guilt, and then outlined the development of the causa sui project, both original and modern. From there, both natural guilt and the drive toward the causa sui project were grounded in the ambiguities of logos and the yearning for authoritative and/or absolute disambiguation. The next chapter, the concluding chapter of Part I, examines the cosmological grounds of logos and guilt. I contextualize the works of both Ernest Becker and Kenneth Burke by more fully exploring the metaphysics of life. To do so, I turn mainly to the philosophical biology of Hans Jonas.

Appendix A:

Kenneth Burke's *"Dialectician's Hymn"*

Hail to Thee, Logos,
Thou Vast Almighty Title,
In Whose name we conjure—
Our acts the partial representatives
Of Thy whole act.

May we be Thy delegates
In parliament assembled.
Parts of Thy wholeness.
And in our conflicts
Correcting one another.
By study of our errors
Gaining Revelation.

May we give true voice
To the statements of Thy creatures.
May our spoken words speak for them,
With accuracy,
That we know precisely their rejoinders
To our utterances,
And so may correct our utterances
In light of those rejoinders.

Thus may we help Thine objects
To say their say—
Not suppressing by dictorial lie,

Not giving false reports
That misrepresent their saying.

If the soil is carried off by flood,
May we help the soil say so.
If our ways of living
Violate the needs of nerve and muscle,
May we find speech for nerve and muscle,
To frame objections
Whereat we, listening,
Can remake our habits.
May we not bear false witness to ourselves
About our neighbors,
Prophesying falsely
Why they did as they did.

May we compete with one another,
To speak for Thy Creation with more justice—
Cooperating in this competition
Until our naming
Gives voice correctly,
And how things are
And how we say things are
Are one.

Let the word be dialectic with the Way—
Whichever the print
The other the imprint.

Above the single speeches
Of things,
Of animals,
Of people
Erecting a speeches-of-speeches—
And above the
A Speech-of-speech-of speeches,
And so on,
Comprehensively,
Until all is headed

In Thy Vast Almighty Title,
Containing implicitly
What in Thy work is drawn out explicitly—
In its plenitude.

And may we have neither the mania of the One
Nor the delirium of the Many—
But both the Union and the Diversity—
The Title and the manifold details that arise
As that Title is restated
In the Narrative of History.

Not forgetting that the Title represents the story's Sequence,
And that the Sequence represents the Power entitled.

For us
Thy Name is a Great Synecdoche
Thy Works a Grand Tautology.

Notes

1   Burke's (1966) chapter "Terministic Screens" suggests that Darwin's screen of continuity prevented recognition of the discontinuities between humans and other animals. Also, it is interesting how Burke (1966), at several different points, discusses Carney and Chein's dispute on the relations between humans and other species of animals.

2   In Buber's terminology we must "itify" the Thou, for we cannot live in the direct I-Thou relation. Natural guilt inheres in taking "it" for the Thou.

3   As Heidegger sums this up: "The human is a being of distance" (1984, 220).

4   See Daniel Dennett's *Elbow Room*, where he discusses the digger wasp, *Sphex ichneumoneus*. Also see *The Parable of the Beast*, where Bleibtreu opens his discussion by examining the wood tick's experience of time-passage. Finally, see Heidegger's (1995) discussion of the differences between plant, animal, and human.

5   Herder (1966) walks though such concerns in his *Origin of Language*.

6   An early and "master work" is his *Theoretical Biology*.

7   Cf. *An Essay on Man*, and in particular his discussion of "the symbol."

8   Dewey's most succinct statements on this matter can be found in his *Experience and Nature*, "Nature, Communication, Meaning." In this chapter Dewey states, "when communication occurs…things reveal themselves not only to man but to themselves."

9   Cf. Langer's chapter "Language."

10 Cf. *The Morning Notes of Adelbert Ames Jr.*

11 Of particular interest are the lectures Heidegger (1995) gave in the early 1930s, particularly those which were informed by his reading of von Uexküll's work. Interested readers should see Heidegger's extended discussion of "dis-inhibiting rings."

12 Cf. *The Phenomenon of Life.*

13 Ong's many works move out of such an orientation, but see, in particular, *The Presence of the Word.*

14 McLuhan (1998, 1964), though not explicitly spelling things out, assumes and takes for granted relations between organismal sensory modalities and spatial/temporal disclosures around them.

15 The intellectual roots go back at least to Herder and then grow significantly with von Uexküll's work.

16 An additional aspect of ambiguous merger and division characterizing the lived-body is the tide flow known as breathing in and breathing out. If I define myself by including all that is necessary for my continuance, then I partly am the air I breathe. Why do we think of lungs as "me" but not the air that we breathe? Alan Watts was fond of asking if you breathe the air or if it breathes you. At any rate, breathing is both more and less than personal; it is semiautonomous.

17 Burke identifies how Spinoza is able to undercut the God/Nature pair without reducing God to nature. He writes,

> The Latin is causa sui, "cause of itself"—and you will note that in this key expression there is both an active and a passive significance...In Spinoza's case... the essence of this active-passive pair is *active*...Hence we see that, in the strategic moment in his God-Nature, or action-motion equation, Spinoza differs from Hobbes in shifting to the action side of the pair. (1962, 140-141)

18 To illustrate, simply observe the ambiguities whereby, "that which was 'a part of' the parent has become 'apart from' the parent; yet it may, from the familial point of view, still be considered consubstantial with its ancestral source" (1962, 406).

19 If, on the contrary, we recognize the ambiguous manners by which we are separate and yet not at all separate, we gain grounds for sufficiently calling into question ethical systems that boil down to: "I should be able to do whatever I want to do as long as my actions do not hurt other people." Better, "less divisive," questions, include: "Even if I personally have not brought harm to another, is it morally wrong if I personally benefit from the harms that someone else brings upon a third party?" And, "Is it a moral failure if I simply refrain from helping another who is in need?" Such questions reveal some of the serious shortcomings in atomistic, visualistic individualism.

20 Sapir, as cited in Langer (1942, 102).

> Many lovers of nature, for instance, do not feel that they truly are in touch with it until they have mastered names of a great many flowers and trees, as though the primary world of reality were a verbal one and as though one could not get close to nature unless one first mastered the terminology which somehow magically expressed it.

21 Readers interested in the difference between logical order and temporal order should see Jonas (1966) on the difference between geometry and modern predicate calculus. Also Cf. Merleau-Ponty (1973) on "The Algorithm and the Mystery of Language."

22 How about the "I" who promises and the "me" who must carry out said promises?

23   As Burke often has noted, "narrative form" and "logical form" can ambiguously change places and thereby transform what are purely logical relations into something of a quasi-narrative structure bearing dramatistic intensity. In *The Rhetoric of Religion*, Burke takes pains to illustrate how logical (eternal) order precipitates into drama when logical orders become temporally enacted. Guilt-cycle analyses thus explore the ways that setting up a covenant, the breaking of that covenant, and the guilt and the means of the repentance/guilt expiation are all logical implicates, eternally logical relations. Nevertheless, our lives, as caught in the throes of finitude, blaze with dramatic light as these logical relations take temporal form. Burke states,

> When we turn from the consideration of a terministic cycle in which the various terms mutually imply on another, to the consideration of the narrative terminology in these opening chapters of Genesis, we note that the narrative terms allow the idea of Order to be "processes." Here one can start with the creation of a natural order (though conceiving it as infused with a verbal principle); one can next proceed to an idea of innocence untroubled by thou-shalt-not's; one can next introduce a thou-shalt-not; one can next depict the thou-shalt-not as violated; one next can depict a new Covenant propounded on the basis of this violation, and with capital punishment; one can later introduce the principle of sacrifice... Then gradually thereafter, more and more clearly, comes the emergence of the turn from mere sacrifice to the idea of outright redemption by victimage... Whereas, the terms of Order, considered tautologically...endlessly implicating one another, when their functions are embodied in narrative style the cycle can be translated into terms of an irreversible linear progression...reduction of the tautological cycle to a narrative linear progression makes possible the notion of an *outcome*. (1961, 216-217)

Here is guilt, in Burke's sense, not as a momentary state of a cycle, but as the *condition* of our existence within any such cycles. Beings who can promise are "point blank" guilty; this is implied in the notions of "persons" and "action."

24   It would be foolhardy to thoroughly disambiguate these. One of the surest ways to bring out the ambiguous nature of merger and division here, and the ways that we are *motivated by* disambiguation, is to understand the nature of terministic screens. Burke's essay addresses those ways that speech, even if reduced to the act of naming or definition, nevertheless leads us; words carry a suasive underbelly because even terminologies that accurately reflect reality must select from that reality and thereby deflect that reality.

25   Burke writes, "Whereas poetic language is a kind of symbolic action, for itself and in itself, and whereas scientific action is preparation for action, rhetorical language is inducement to action (or to attitude, attitude being an incipient act)" (1962, 566).

26   Although animals have incredibly sophisticated and complex sign-systems, we find little evidence that other creatures make denotative propositions, or talk *about* the world per se (cf. Bateson 1972).

27   Cf. Arthur Koestler, in his *The Ghost in the Machine* (1967, 44-53).

28   Burke (1966, 370-371) addresses these issues, suggesting that his insights are indebted to, though they take a more dramatistic read than, the ideas first explored by Berkeley and Bentham.

29 My focus on "structure" and "function" is highly indebted to Hugh Dalziel Duncan who, in my opinion, reads Burke exceptionally well. He is able, as so few are, to grasp the forest, not merely various trees along the way. He succeeds better than most in avoiding undue reduction to the whole of Burke's ideas.

30 Cf. Anton (2001).

31 "...the contracting and expanding of scene is rooted in the very nature of linguistic placement" (1962, 84).

32 "'Order' *as such*," the young Burke argues, "makes for a tangle of guilt, mystery, ambition ('adventure') and vindication that infuses even the most visible and tangible of material 'things' with the spirit of the order through which they are perceived" (1954, 288).

33 "The *Rhetoric* deals with the possibilities of classification in its partisan aspects... The *Rhetoric* must lead us through the Scramble, the Wrangle of the Market Place, the flurries and flare-ups of the human Barnyard, the Give and Take, the wavering line of pressure and counterpressure, the Logomachy, the onus of ownership, the Wars of Nerves, the War...For one need not scrutinize the concept of 'identification' very sharply to see, implied in it at every turn, its ironic counterpart: division" (Burke 1962, 546-547).

34 "The notion of 'rights' in nature is a quasi-naturalistic, metaphysical subterfuge for sanctioning in apparently biological terms a state of affairs that is properly discussed in terms specifically suited to the treatment of symbolism as motive" (Burke 1954, 275).

35 We are not inevitably driven to violence. On the contrary, we are admonished, as Burke's (1982) John O Neal might say, to "watch your mind as you'd eye a mean dog."

36 The fuzzy boundary where differences "in degree" become differences "in kind" is nicely displayed in the drift from *possession* to *ownership*. Possession, arguably, is universal to all animals. They claim the ground upon which they walk or purchase a position that physically occupies space. Talons, claws, paws, and arms, all of these are capable of some kind of possession. But can I own something without knowing that I possess it? Ownership, it would seem, is a symbolic enterprise, which is sanctified not by immediately exerted force of defense, but by the secret sign of negativity, "not yours." Ownership is a metonymy of possession, but one that is not necessarily related to consumption or direct use. It is often for display. Animals do not own in this regard. Granted they certainly can possess as long as they can defend. But ownership is so different than this. It is backed by an authority that is neither animal nor, strictly speaking, visible. Future consideration might be given to the key differences between the concept of "belongings" and the concept of "possessions."

37 Toward the end of *A Rhetoric of Motives*, Burke writes,

> Thus one particular order (or property structure), with its brands of "mystery," may be better suited than another for the prevailing circumstances. Hence, to say that hierarchy is inevitable is not to argue categorically against a new order on the grounds that it would but replace under one label what had been removed under another. It is merely to say that, in any order, there will be the mysteries of hierarchy, since such a principle is grounded in the very nature of language... The intensities, morbidities, or particularities of mystery come from institutional

sources, but the *aptitude* comes from the nature of man, generically, as a *symbol-using animal.* (1962, 803)

38 In *A Grammar of Motives*, Burke explicitly calls for a neo-Stoic cosmopolitanism at three different points (1962, 318; 442-443).

39 Even though his appropriations were in fact quite sparse, Becker gives considerable praise to Kenneth Burke. In fact, he cites Burke in two books, once in *Beyond Alienation* and several times in *Escape from Evil*. Burke's writings do not mention Becker, and Burke may not even have been familiar with Becker's work. Still, one cannot help but wonder how Burke would have placed Becker. Clearly, both have strong ties to Nietzsche and Freud, and both share a concern over guilt and sacrifice. Still, Burke would likely have been much more critical of Becker's scientific reductions. All this, but I do not think that Burke would have been that critical of Becker's project.

40 He is not alone is this regard. Numerous brilliant minds have underestimated both the naturalness of speech as well as its properly spiritual office. For a line that has not underestimated it see Stahmer (1968).

41 In *The Denial of Death*, Becker writes, "What does it mean to be a *self-conscious animal*? The idea is ludicrous, if it is not monstrous...This is the terror: to have emerged from nothing, to have a name, consciousness of self, deep inner feelings, an excruciating inner yearning for life and self-expression—and with all of this yet to die. It seems like a hoax, which is why one type of cultural man rebels openly against the idea of God. What kind of deity would create such complex and fancy worm food" (1973, 87).

42 "All told, in this project directed 'towards the purification of war,' the *Grammar* should assist to this end through encouraging tolerance by speculation...we may hope at least to temper the extreme rawness of our ambitions, once we become aware of the ways in which we are the victims of our own and another's magic. Such, then, are 'moralistic' reasons for the enterprise. They are offered in the firm belief that a kind of 'Neo-Stoic resignation' to the needs of industrial expansion is in order" (Burke 1962, 442).

Self-preservation, physio-chemical identity,
pulsating body warmth,
a sense of power and satisfaction in activity
—all these tally up in symbolic man
to the emergence of the heroic urge.
(Becker 1971, 76-77)

"Actually, 'final causes' are not futural at all but continually present (a kind of nunc stans) until attained or abandoned."
(Burke 1961, 246)

CHAPTER 3

THE COSMOLOGICAL GROUNDS OF LOGOS

Many people in the modern Western world feel that they ought to be a self-cause. They believe in the obligation to think for themselves, and they feel pressure to make something of themselves. They understand themselves reflexively and have assumed the authority, at least to some degree, for self-governance. How did it come to this? How were persons enabled to presume that as individuals, or even as individuals forming publics, they should own such responsibility?

This question, a query into the various historical sources of the modern *causa sui* project, was already addressed in chapter 1. Here I simply recall that for Ernest Becker the main source was symbol-use coupled with money and linear calendars. From time-immemorial, cyclical rituals of worldly rejuvenation came slowly to be modified by modern notions of "linear time," and moreover, accruals of compound interest and various material and technological innovations gave more and more reality to the notion of an autonomous, freestanding, individual.[1] For Kenneth Burke, too, it was symbolicity and money, and also the ways and means of technological innovation whereby humans were "separated from their natural conditions by instruments of their own making."[2] Additional support for both Becker and Burke comes from the analyses of Georg Simmel in his monumental *The Philosophy of Money*. Simmel reveals how monetary forms were necessary not only for the objectification of value in human experience, but also for releasing individuals from any particular collective. In brief, money makes "the stranger" functionally possible. For Walter J. Ong literacy seems to have made all the difference in freeing up the resources of interiority and in facilitating the development of self-reflexive individuals. Perhaps more clearly and extensively than any other thinker, Ong documents how the emergence of personalism and the reach of outward objectification ran in conjunction with historical developments in communication technologies. Diverse as these thinkers are, all have identified sociohistorical factors that actualized the experience of individuation and extended the reach of outward transcendence. Money and literacy serve precisely these ends. They were crucial to the kinds of technological innovation that made individualistic anonymity fully functional and ever expanding in its possibilities. As the two legs upon which the modern causa sui project walks, they are the forms of mediation that enable people to cover-over the unending ambiguity of existence and their own natural guilt.[3] They are part of the attempt at an impossible heroism, one that would be beyond the need of expiation.

Heroism without expiation, I have been suggesting, becomes possible only where money and literacy already are found, and so, modern individuals, people who literally pay for what they own, easily imagine themselves as fully and completely self-made—as if from the bottom up. If asked about natural guilt, they neither consciously feel it nor do they explicitly yearn to expiate it. But this does not mean that moderns have successfully become self-causes nor does it mean that they have extirpated the roots of natural guilt. Despite the many life horizons where the sense of the causa sui project prevails, ambiguity always remains: earthquake, flood, fire, lightning bolt, brain aneurism, or other kinds of crisis can be only moments away.

Throughout the previous two chapters, I addressed the theme of individuation as well as explored the nature and scope of human transcendence. The task taken up in the present chapter is to show how the seeds of the causa sui project were metaphysically sown. As the final chapter of Part I, this analysis complements and contextualizes the previous discussion by turning to the philosophical biology of Hans Jonas. Jonas's speculative cosmology details various continuities and discontinuities between inorganic matter, metabolic and cellular life, vegetative life, animality, and human existence, focusing on the ever-developing forms of mediation (i.e., expanding horizons of merger and division as well as individuation and transcendence). His work provides ample resources for tracing the fullest expression of the causa sui project all the way back to its beginning in the very development of organic life out from inorganic matter. Life *per se* seems to have embarked on the venture of becoming more individuated and self-aware and opening thereby to wider and greater risks. The cosmos itself, therefore, is guilty of having made logos possible; it bears the weight of having enabled the drive toward the experience of individuation, a physically and materially doomed individuation, which nonetheless holds the possibility of expanding modes of transcendence.

Jonas's overall sketch gives solid support to Becker's claim that, "the development of life is life's own burden" (1975, 34). We are not, therefore, either socially or personally the source of natural guilt. The universe itself is guilty of having released itself into the ambiguous and perilous odyssey of selfhood, and we are merely sites of the guilt naturally encumbered. The critical implication for this study, I will try to show, regards the possibility of learning how to forgive the universe for individuating itself, one's own case in particular. We can thereby learn to engage in heroic expiations, rituals of worldly rejuvenation that meditate upon the Eternal and give grateful forgiveness to the mysterious powers from which our lives emerged and upon which they ambiguously depend.

Cosmological Grounds for Logos

Kenneth Burke argues that the origin of language is no less mysterious than is the origin of the universe itself. Both, he suggests, are simply "the given." This is a shrewd insight, but a residual challenge for Burke is that he also maintains a discontinuity between human action and the motions of mere things that pervade the rest of the natural world.[4] He thus posits a distinction between the "action" of persons and the "motion" of things, and it is here, precisely, that we might want to invite Hans Jonas into the parlor.

Evolving Mediacies: Dialectics of Freedom and Necessity

It is common practice, and so a major temptation, to curtail the phenomenon of freedom to the realms of human decisions and action. But the initial leap from absolute necessity to evolving dialectics of freedom/necessity can be shown to begin, not with the emergence of symbol-use per se, but rather with the emergence of metabolic processes and the development of organic life amidst and atop inorganic matter.[5] Summarizing a vast evolutionary progression—one that cosmologically contextualizes the sociohistorical developments of logos—Jonas writes,

> The great contradictions that man discovers in himself—freedom and necessity, autonomy and dependence, ego and world, connectedness and isolation, creativity and mortality—are present *in nuce* in life's more primitive forms, each of which maintains a perilous balance between being and nonbeing and from the very beginning harbors within itself an inner horizon of "transcendence." This theme, common to all life, can be traced in its development through the ascending order of organic capabilities and functions: metabolism, motility and appetite, feeling and perception, imagination, art, and thinking—a progressive scale of freedom and danger, reaching its pinnacle in man, who can perhaps understand his uniqueness in a new way if he no longer regards himself in metaphysical isolation. (1996, 60)

The freedom of symbolic action (i.e., logos as language, discourse, or eidetic image) may be discontinuous with the movements of inorganic matter, but this does not mean that it is discontinuous with the rest of the living universe. In fact, if we wish to discover where the articulate logos becomes precast as a possibility we must trace its ancestry all the way back to the beginning of the phenomenon of life. As we do so, we find resources for reinterpreting the underlying drive that has sociohistorically come to fruition as self-esteem, heroism, and ultimately, the modern causa sui project.

Metabolism and Vegetation

Inorganic identity is characterized by sheer presence without relational inwardness or outwardness, and its own continuance does not require incorporations that metabolize ingested elements from the surrounding environment. It neither needs to reproduce nor can it. In these regards, inorganic matter seems to accomplish a kind of selfsame permanence that life itself, an endless ebb and tide of ambiguous mergers and divisions, remains unable to achieve. And, as Jonas suggests, "If mere assurance of permanence were the point that mattered, life should not have started out in the first place" (1966, 106).

Life is inherently risk: it principally separates off an identity from the temporary material that passes through it but upon which it depends. Metabolism, the first order of *mediacy*, the first order of pulsating merger and division, represents a leap that liberates into peril, for life always encumbers the continued threat of non-being within its being.[6] In this profound sense, the mystery regarding the origin of the universe inheres in why life would emerge out of the assured and safe continuance of inorganic presence. Indeed, life emerges only at a hefty price, first the ongoing possibility of death and then its inescapability in the end. To such costs we are compelled to ask: How is this risky venture fulfilled in return? The gain is perhaps quite obvious: life offers the possibility of transcendence.[7] The two horizons of transcendence that the mediacy of life makes possible are space and time. Time, here referring to the concatenated phases of its own growth and development, and space, referring to the continuous and contiguous surround upon which any form of life depends for nutritive commerce.

Metabolism and cellular boundaries make possible a kind of division that dialectically holds resources for now merging with the outer environment with greater range and scope. Organic wholes maintain a dependence upon and an independence from the matter that passes through them. Consider a tomato plant. It grows as if producing its own branches and making its own fruit, but it does not create the matter that it or the fruit is made of. The identities of life, metabolic tissues, operate atop the eternally undead world of matter.[8] Compared to the sheer selfsame identity of matter, the identity of vegetative life is characterized by increased dimensions of inwardness and extended outward freedom. Granted that almost all land plants are rooted to the earth, meaning that they are without the kind of visible individuation that characterizes animal life and admittedly are without sensory organs or the possibility of motility, plant life opens to the proximal and hence is quite limited in its modes of transcendence. Nonetheless, vegetative mediation marks a significant leap beyond the inorganic. It enables and constrains plants to grow, turn toward light, take in and give off gasses, vie with neighboring vegetation for territorial expansion, reproduce, and finally, die.

Note also that unlike replication by simple cell division, plant processes of reproduction and fertilization are sexual and interactive with the larger world. They are perhaps the farthest reaches of spatial transcendence that are possible for plant life. Nonetheless, they remain utterly blind and anonymous—often involve indifferent intermediaries—and are without the opportunities, necessities, or agonies of attraction displays, mating rituals, and/or courting processes.

Animality

Characterized by greater degrees of outwardness and inward differentiation than plant life, animal life extends the scope and range of outwardly directed concern and radically expands the horizons of spatial and temporal experience. When compared to plant life, which is without distant desires, animality reveals a temporal dimension (e.g., a chase, or the anxiety of frustrated movement). Some feeling of temporal duration and orientation accompanies the experience of distance that sensory organs make possible. Admittedly, when compared to the temporal expanses to which humans open, the temporal transcendence of animal life may appear quite limited, but we need to underscore that the difference in range of spatial mediacy is the most noticeable difference between plant life and animal life.[9] As Jonas suggests, "it is the main characteristic of animal evolution as distinct from plant life that space, as the dimension of dependence, is progressively transformed into a dimension of freedom by the parallel evolution of these two powers: to move about, and to perceive at a distance" (1966, 100). Animals transcend the physical, visible boundaries of their flesh, for sensory organs open awareness to distant desires as well as distant threats. Second, animal life transcends space by powers of motility and movement; not only able to perceive distant food and predators, they are able to rove about. They often claim a territory, as if marking off the range of their spatial horizons. They also are able to attempt to flee from detected and approaching predators.[10] Taken all together, motility and perception are inseparable from the realms of feeling that animals are capable of; dogs and higher mammals are highly emotive and can be filled with organismal anxieties in ways that plant life seems not to be.[11]

Animals need mates for reproduction, and throughout the animal kingdom we find a wide array of courtship processes and mating practices. Far transcending the deaf and blind anonymity of plant reproduction, a world without "alpha" displays or "sexual selection," some higher mammals evince a considerable amount preference in their sexual behavior (i.e., they show evidence of onymous or "choosey" differentiation).

Compared to the rather limited—and that also means safe—horizons of vegetative mediation, animal mediacy is fraught with increased possibilities of blockage and other forms of resistance. The development of sensory organs, the capacity for powers of locomotion, and the realm of affect all make possible appetites and desires that are as much subject to satisfaction as they are to frustration and elusion. And the very principle of animal life, roving individuation, is rather horrific in its implications: organismal parturition creates physically isolated mortal entities that not only desire and need distant and possibly scarce food for survival, but some of the animals live by devouring the other ones. As Jonas suggests, "Its enjoyments has suffering as its shadow side, its loneliness the compensation of communication: the gain lies not on either side of the balance sheet but in the togetherness of both i.e. in the enhancement of that selfhood with which 'organism' originally dared indifferent nature" (1966, 107).

What becomes obvious is that any adequate evaluation of life itself must reckon with the dialectics of mediation that pervade the universe on an evolutionary scale. Increased risks and dependency, greater possibilities of failure and frustration, these are the prices paid for expanded ranges of freedom. At each stage of expanding mediation, costs and risks are encumbered for the sake of possible fulfillments.[12]

> This increased mediacy buys greater scope, internal and external, at the price of greater hazard, internal and external. A more pronounced self is set over against a more pronounced world...The rift between subject and object, which long-range perception and motility opened and which the keenness of appetite and fear, of satisfaction and disappointment, of pleasure and pain, reflect, was never to be closed again. But in its widening expanse the freedom of life found room for all those modes of relation—perception, active and emotional—which in spanning the rift justify it and by indirection redeem the lost unity. (Jonas 1966, 107)

The guiding principle underneath these many different evolutionary developments is elegant and clear: a mediating boundary enables both inwardness and outwardness, freedom coupled with necessity. And so, animal mediacy paves the way for even greater degrees of transcendence, and from this we are led to the fullest—meaning the chanciest—of all mediations: humanity and the highly articulate logos known as speech and/or symbolic action.

Humanity

Humanity is continuous with animality, as it is with all of life, but the range and scope of human transcendence turns a difference of degree into a difference in kind. The human use of tools, and use of tools for using and making tools, has served as a traditional way of marking this difference. *Homo faber*, the toolmaker, does seem to designate, at least partly, what is distinctly human. The skillful use of tools to make projectile weaponry offers a vivid illustration of expanded and articulated spatial transcendence. By throwing a spear or shooting an arrow, humans extend their range of action while also refining the accuracy of their reach. Consider too that humans have technologically equipped and outfitted themselves to survive in almost any territory. But interpreted this way, humans seem to have amplified merely the scope and efficiency of spatial mediacy, and if it were merely the radical extension and honing of such spatial transcendence that marked humanity, we might not be justified in calling it a difference *in kind*.

The point to be brought out here is that tool construction and tool use already presuppose forms of eidetic, pictorial, and temporal transcendence. The earliest rudiments of human conceptualization can be found in the sheer capability of detachedly arresting objects in view, blankly staring at them as if they were neutralized for inspection.[13] To hold still and look at something is to maintain an image of that thing despite the fact that only partial profiles of it are given at any instant. This leads Jonas to suggest that sight, "of all senses, most conspicuously realizes in its normal performance this double feat of 'abstraction': setting off the self-contained object from the affective condition of sensing, and upholding its identity and unity across the whole range of its possible transformation of appearance" (1966, 168).[14] Vision thus separates an eidetic image from the thing looked at and involves the possibility of detached survey, and we find the fullest human conceptual capacities, including powers of abstraction, categorization, and the appetite for some notion of truth, to be given first form in the human way of looking at objects in the surrounding world.[15] The possible discovery of the concept of a circle, for example, is precast by the ability to wean an eidetic image out from immediate sensory experience.

But the range of human mediations involved is not limited to the ways that humans *see* the world uniquely, regardless of whether or not conceptualization is largely unavailable to animals. Humanity is distinguished not only by the natural generation of eidetic images out from the sensory surround, but also by the fact that images can come under the conscious control of an imagining person and serve as a guide for articulate hand movements. The uniquely human ability to draw, however crude or inept the drawings, shows evidence of movements guided by images that have been arrested out of the sensory flux of immediate experience. And such pictorial representation embodies an even further level of mediation: *image-making*.

> What we have here is a trans-animal, uniquely human fact: eidetic control of motility, that is, muscular action governed not by set stimulus-response pattern but by freely chosen, internally represented and purposefully projected form. The eidetic control of motility, with its freedom of external execution, complements the eidetic control of imagination, with its freedom of internal drafting...*homo pictar* represented the point in which *homo faber* and *homo sapiens* are conjoined—are indeed shown to be one and the same. (Jonas 1966, 172-173)

In outlining the distinguishing characteristics of humanity we found a unique level of conceptual mediation: an abstract and malleable eidos interposes itself between sense organs and the perceived world. Humans have therefore ceased to interact with the environment in an immediate way and have learned to encounter the world through eidetic images and to guide and direct movements accordingly. Moreover, to this mode of eidetic mediation, we soon enough find an even further emergent form: the development of reflexive objectification, where the self confronts itself with the burden of mediacy and opens itself to a self-mediating relation.

People everywhere around the globe construct an image of what and how a person is supposed to be. They also subject themselves, whether they wish to or not, to self judgments in comparison to that image. All of this leads Jonas to write,

> In reflection upon self the subject-object split which began to appear in animal evolution reaches its extreme form. It has extended into the center of feeling life, which is now divided against itself. Only over the immeasurable distance of being his own object can man "have" himself. ...As in all achievements of life, the price is high. As human satisfaction is different from animal and far surpassing its scope, so is human suffering, though man also shares in the animal range of feelings. But only man can be happy and unhappy, thanks to the measuring of his being against terms that transcend the immediate situation. Supremely concerned with what he is, how he lives, what he makes out of himself, and viewing himself from the distance of his wishes, aspirations, and approvals, man and man alone is open to despair. (1966, 186)

The unique form of freedom that humans bear comes from having to live with the agonizing and fulfilling possibilities that are encumbered with self-reflexive temporal openness. Human freedom is that form of mediation that, reflexive to itself, encumbers responsibility; it is the place of the universe where modes of mediated transcendence are so perfected that they enable abstract self-mediation. We find an interior "I," a boundary of inwardness separated from even the body and that seems thereby open to the most transcendent realms of inward imagination.

Human expanses of temporal transcendence also include the possibility running ahead of oneself to ultimate ends, understanding the inevitability of one's own death (Heidegger 1993). And here, with the notion of one's own end, the very telos that is one's life, we come upon the final distinguishing characteristic of humanity, a mediation unique to the human species: responsibility.

The Cosmological Ground for the Causa Sui Project

The grand narrative told above, at least for many people, raises critical questions about teleology and purpose. People may feel compelled to ask why the universe has made possible the experience of responsibility. They also might want to go back to the earlier question of why life emerged in the first place. Why did matter embark on the project of opening itself to greater degrees of risk and enjoyment, especially given that death was set as both an ever-present possibility and as the ultimate inevitability? What is the meaning of all this? *How are we to understand the purpose of these various reaches of mediation given their inevitable ends?* And what could be the possible purpose of human transcendence? In a word, "*why humanity?*" Why has such responsibility (such openness to the fullest senses of inwardness, outwardness, and existential particularity) become possible? For what possible end could humans have been sentenced to dwell in such robust modes of recollective and anticipative responsibility?[16]

Perhaps obviously, life itself might have occurred without any reason, and so, there may be no "purpose" to life at all. It might be a purposeless fact standing without any sense or reason; it could be a metaphysical and cosmological accident. Even more possibly, questions beginning with the word, "Why" are simply beyond the scope of the natural and biological sciences. They hold no possibility of scientific testing, verification, or falsification. But regardless of whether a response is beyond science, and, even if life is "fluke," many people, in living their lives, do seem to need some kind of meaningful answer nonetheless. The bulk of the modern Western world not only finds the question "why humanity?" to be intelligible, many people around the globe have a rough and ready response. Major lines of response take shape around some notions of "judgment" and/or the "afterlife." Numerous religious traditions suggest that human responsibility is tied into possibilities of "life eternal," "reincarnation," and/or "personal salvation at the end of the world."

Jonas, for his own account, is not without a response to these concerns. We find him spinning a cosmic myth, one that issues an ultimately heroic horizon for human ends. Jonas puts the range of life's progressions and developments into an ultimate perspective by proposing that in the proverbial "beginning," the Divine allowed the cosmos to come into being, though the energy that was required to initiate the task exhausted the divine's powers. The Eternal ground of being was therefore able to begin creation, offering but the possibility of various levels of ambiguous mergers and divisions that could serve as forcing beds for transcendence, but the act was so demanding that it liquidated all omniscience and omnipotence.[17] Describing the impulse of this original creation, Jonas writes:

> In order that the world might be, and be for itself, God renounced his own being, divesting himself of his deity—to receive it back from the Odyssey of time weighted with the chance harvest of unforeseeable temporal experience: transfigured or possibly even disfigured by it. In such self-forfeiture of divine integrity for the sake of unprejudiced becoming, no other foreknowledge can be admitted than that of *possibilities* which cosmic being offers in its own terms: to these, God committed his cause in effacing himself for the world... Having given himself whole to the becoming world, God has no more to give: it is man's now to give to him. (1966, 275-279)

Further elaborating on this idea, Jonas argues that humans were made not *in* the image of God but rather *for* God's image. This means that the extra-mundane register for human actions is not a book that will list the evidence used to gain or deny entrance for "personal salvation" in some kind of afterlife. On the contrary, human deeds take their ultimate transcendence in their extra-mundane releasement of the divine countenance:

> God's own destiny, his doing or undoing, is at stake in this universe to whose unknowing dealings he committed his substance, and man has become the eminent repository of this supreme and ever betrayable trust. In a sense, he holds the fate of the deity in his hands...Thus...the image of God, haltingly begun by the universe, for so long worked upon—and left undecided—in the wide and then narrowing spirals of pre-human life, passes with this last twist, and with a dramatic quickening of the movement, into man's precarious trust, to be completed, saved, or spoiled by what he will do to himself and the world. And in this awesome impact of his deeds on God's destiny, on the very complexion of eternal being, lies the immortality of man. (Jonas 1966, 274-277)

Humans have been sentenced to the responsibility of giving form to the Eternal's visage. Three interrelated points deserve address here: first, the ground of being, by Jonas's account, sentenced itself to the fate of chance, to decisions made within the unfolding contingencies of finitude. This implies that the Divine has been divested of divinity and lies vulnerable and in eternal peril. As Jonas suggests, "the deity held nothing back of itself: no uncommitted or unimpaired part remained to direct, correct, and ultimately guarantee the devious working-out of its destiny in creation" (1966, 275). Second, just as the Divine is without any resources to ensure the ultimate outcomes of existence, so too humans lack the benefit of any further divine intervention.[18] They only can rely upon their transcendence, their temporal openness, the finite freedom they have to make decisions. Third, the two points just mentioned dovetail in the fact that the deity itself encumbered a particular kind of peril: to be left without a face. And here we come upon the special reason—the extra-mundane reason—for human levels of mediation. We bear the responsibility for consummating the very face of the Divine, and so, it is not really surprising that humanity opens to kinds of transcendence that incorporate images of perfection (also cf. Anton 2010).

Though he does not elaborate upon them, Jonas offers some insightful closing remarks, observations that point in the direction I would like to go. He concludes that:

> the secret sympathy that connects our being with the transcendent condition and makes the latter depend upon our deeds, must somehow work both ways…If so, the state of transcendence, as we have let it become, will in turn have a resonance in ours—sometimes felt, though mostly not, and presently felt, perhaps in a general malaise, in the profound distemper of the contemporary mind… (1966, 280)

Jonas here suggests that our acts not only bear upon the Divine's face, but, indirectly, they likewise bear upon the "temper of the times" into which persons find themselves. Even more generally cast, Jonas's implied response to the question, "why humanity?" avoids an appeal to personal salvation in two directions. First, people have been entrusted as stewards to the Divine's odyssey through time, and hence human freedom is granted so that God's image may openly shape itself within the situated contingencies of choice and action. Second, marks upon the Eternal have an indirect impact upon those currently within historical existence. This is experienced, even if "mostly not felt," as the "spirit" of the times. We might even speculate that the power and strength of the causa sui project is inversely proportionate to the felt strength of the Divine. For millennia in the Western tradition, the earliest humans could only imagine and experience an all-powerful, wrathful, and vengeful god. And then, for two thousand years people believed in a powerful but all-loving and forgiving God. Now, today, we are at the beginning of a new era, an era of the impotent, vulnerable, and incomplete God, a Deity who depends upon our help.[19]

Granting a wealth of provocation here, let me now develop one aspect of Jonas's depiction that I would slightly problematize and modify. Unfortunately, both the popular notion of "the afterlife" and even Jonas's mystical account maintain that humanity is for something other than life; the main and primary register for human transcendence is something outside of life per se. Whereas the popular "afterlife" account grounds responsible freedom in its bearing on the judgment and the state of the soul after the death of the body,[20] Jonas's mystical account casts the meaning of responsibility as it bears upon the visage of the Eternal. In that regard, both positions seem to appeal to a reason or purpose that is transcendent to the phenomenon of life.[21] Both make transcendence a means rather than the ends of life per se.

Rather than commit to a grand teleological story of evolution, or suggest that the cosmos itself yearned for more inward self-definition and greater transcendence outward, we can simply identify a logical rather than temporal progression. We accordingly focus only on the "logical development" that seems evident in the continuities and discontinuities between the inorganic, the cellular and metabolic, the vegetative, the animal, and the uniquely human. Furthermore, even if we stand in ignorance of how such developments of organic mediacy have become what they are today, (they may well have emerged as sheer fluke), we must acknowledge that we do experience some kind of teleology in the human realm. Human actions unquestionably take their form by movements toward consciously chosen ends. To be human is to be open to final causes, meaning that we are the part of nature that self-consciously experiences final causes. The mere feel of the material world's resistance against my actions, pedestrian as this example is, offers a metaphysical disclosure of something resembling "the will." And promises too—including those we make to ourselves and those that we fail to keep—exemplify the teleological nature of human action. In offering and then committing to a promise, humans dwell in the freedom that is responsibility. These highly developed experiences of freedom, the levels of freedom that make love possible, are part of the human experience of willing, striving, and openness to past and future. Hence, by recognizing that humans are continuous with the natural world—part of nature rather than an alien presence temporarily trapped within it—we come to find a place in nature where teleology is hard to deny.

Can we imagine, then, a position that would roughly support Jonas's philosophical biology but that would not make any appeal to a realm that is other than of this world? Can we come to grasp that life itself is sacred and is its own why (also cf. Scheler 1961). Is it possible to understand the why of human mediations—thereby giving words and human deeds a kind of extra-mundane significance—without endorsing a significance that is other than in and for life?

It is perhaps worth recalling that Jonas begins his myth by stating, "In the beginning, for unknowable reasons, the ground of being, or the Divine, chose to give itself over to the chance and risk and endless variety of becoming" (1966, 275). His opening holds the problematic anachronism; it places God into existence before existence began. But I can better address this point from a different angle: Jonas suggests that our lives "trace lines in the divine countenance." What a beautiful and captivating expression. And how intriguing, the idea that God was able to create all but his visage. But, and here is what I wish to challenge, for the Eternal as Eternal this story makes little sense. We need, on the contrary, to find room for a theistic naturalism, or a naturalistic theism. The challenge is to open a biologically-grounded spirituality, one that is genuinely extra-mundane but that is sufficiently pruned of delusions, fantasies, and fairy-tale endings of the "happily-ever-after" sort.

Reinterpreting the Meaning of Mortality

So many people in the modern Western world, especially many contemporary Christians who loudly claim to feel God's love, do not genuinely know how to love. Because they misunderstand the cosmological roots of the causa sui project and the meaning of their individuation, their inwardness and uniqueness becomes but the means to hold themselves (and sometimes others) hostage. Even if only unwittingly, they attempt an emotional and pseudo-intellectual blackmail: they make up a bunch of self-serving fantasies, put those into a projected God's silent and unseen mouth, and then act as if doing their part of the deal obligates "God" to deliver on his side of the arrangement. The covenant becomes a kind of ransom to be paid. Basically unable to forgive the Mystery for enabling them to imagine more than they can have, such people are basically selfish. Seriously, if you were to ask the average Christian on the street today if they can forgive God, most would likely say, "Forgive God? You don't forgive God! God is all-good and all-loving and perfect." But what if the Divine actually does need deep and profound human forgiveness, maybe even rituals of forgiveness? What if, as paradoxical as it first sounds, God has no one but us to expiate his guilt?

Not only did no one ask to be born, but there very likely is not a life after this one. What if, just for the sake of argument, there is only this world. It admittedly includes other people, sunshine, shade, breezes, tasty fruits, paintings, music, butterflies, orgasms, and rainbows, but *there is no life after death*. If people knew this to be the case, how many could forgive the cosmos and say, "That is well enough; I am still thankful and grateful." On the contrary, how many would basically prefer some form of atheism to belief in a God unable to bestow immortality?[22]

A sure sign of maturity is learning to forgive our parents as well as to thank them. Our sense of gratitude grows, in fact, only where we are able to forgive. If more people could understand the meaning of individuation and transcendence, they might be able to properly address the Mystery. Embracing a neo-Stoic heroism of death acceptance, they might even say, *"The cosmos couldn't give me immortality, but could offer only the possibility of contemplating perfections that are always in reach but beyond realization, and also a shared world that will continue on after my death, and all of this is good."* In such open gratitude, without any resentment toward death, we say, "yes" to life. We learn to forgive God for being unable to grant eternal personal salvation, and therein we feel thrilled that we received an invitation to the ambiguous feast.

I now offer for your reflection the following summary account: The universe somehow has the possibility for part of itself to appropriate varying degrees of the rest of itself in the mode of self-estrangement and thereby reunite with itself on higher and higher planes of contact. Each of us is a part of that.[23] We need to understand ourselves as symptoms of a cosmic attempt to create the paradox by which, if only ambiguously and temporarily, matter could experience itself as freed from its dependence of being wholly itself as it is. This cosmologically created the possibility of an ambiguous and guilty being. Because of the range and scope of human transcendence, we are agonizingly more and less than what we are. Fundamentally *of* matter but beyond it nonetheless, more than the pulsating identity of continuance across difference provided by metabolic processes, more than the horizons of perception, motility, and feeling, humans are that part of the universe that is able to distinguish itself as "I," that part where consciousness can dwell upon the infinite, the perfect, and the eternal. In this sense, "By transcending animality while at the same time remaining bound to it, man is regarded as the citizen of two worlds, as midway between animal and angel—in short, as a partly supernatural being rising above nature, even animate nature" (Jonas 1996, 76). We are transcending beings, and our transcendence offers a kind of subdivinity, but none of this ever leaves worldly life. The task at hand, then, is to recover some sense of final cause without falling into what might be called the "trap of teleology." The trap reduces both life and human existence to a kind of puzzle whose meaning is to be found other than in life, which inadvertently has the cumulative effect of trivializing and even degrading life's sacredness. The trap of teleology assumes that transcendence is a mere means to an end, not an end in and for life itself.[24]

Let me make this very clear. If we look only to the range and levels of mediation that are found throughout the cosmos, we can identify, if only roughly, three different kinds of Being. Each kind offers a mode of identity that exhibits a significantly different spatial and temporal character than the others. They range from the "self-same identity of matter," to the many modes of "organic continuance in all its varieties" including human modes of mediation, to those particular eidetic identities, those "eternal veracities" such as "pi" that have been disclosed by human powers of transcendence.

Let me say more about these three basic modes of being: *First* is the "Never Was," that which *is* but manifests only as present, never as *was*. One might think of the sheer position and motion of inorganic matter; that which is only and always where and when it is as it is. The "Never Was," therefore, refers to the continued selfsame identity that, as such, is without any time-tenses other than a sheer "*becoming* present." It is the mode of being that is so thoroughly a becoming that it is forever new, meaning "Never Was." The exemplar of the Never Was in the human realm is the indexical level of symbolicity and language use. It is the living voice, the voice that is a cry more than a denotative word.

Second is the "Indefinitely Ongoing," the ambiguously continuing that stretches along, tarries, and elongates in various aporia-filled forms of retention, anticipation, and repetition. We here can identify of all of the various stages of mediation that characterize all forms and levels of *life*. To varying degrees all forms of life experience some retentional sense of "was" and some degree of protentional "not yet." We here might think of the many different actions or discursive activities, the gathering places and moments of human life. The exemplar of the "Indefinitely Ongoing" is the stretching along of culture made possible by speech, handicrafts, and material culture.

Third is the "Beyond all Tenses," also known as "The Eternal," that which is neither continuing nor fleeting, but outside of all passage, outside of all presence or absence. The Eternal, being outside of all becoming, is not the selfsame identity of matter. The exemplar of The Eternal is the abstract *form*, the eidetic image that transcends all particular matter and empirical instantiation.

In sum: The Eternal can enter existence only from within the human range of mediation. On its own terms, *unmediated*, it is too similar to the "Never Was." Only in the perfection of the second mode (i.e., by human transcendence) can the first and third be divided out from each other. As the "Ambiguously Transcendent Place and Moment of the Indefinitely Ongoing " humans are the mediating gateway between the Never Was and The Eternal; only when humans are can The Eternal be parceled out from what Never Was.

Closing Remarks

Two threads pull together the bulk of the previous chapters and capture what fundamentally unites the ideas of Ernest Becker, Kenneth Burke, and Hans Jonas. First and foremost, all three thinkers were highly dissatisfied with the growing trends of naturalistic (i.e., non-transcendent) scientific reductionisms. Each arguably sought some kind of biologically-friendly theology. Second, all three recognized and traded upon some notion of teleology, some notion of *purpose*, even if such purpose becomes self-reflexive or conscious only at the level or stage of humanity. This further means that all three thinkers provided entire worldviews that challenge naive Darwinian reductionisms; all three have sought to recover the fullest sense of human action by considering possible relations to divine action.[25]

In contrast to what I have been suggesting is a weak notion of transcendence—the kind of transcendence that is imagined in the popular account of the afterlife—I have tried to outline more powerful and robust forms. I now conclude this chapter by reviewing three overlapping horizons of transcendence. Each offers vibrant possibilities for rejuvenating action and heroic expiation.

The first horizon refers to the possibilities of one's own most self-cultivation, and at this level of analysis, each person's life-journey is the why of human life. The why is answered by the sheer ability to grow and develop oneself according to an image of who one ought to be. This is not the growth that simply occurs, but the fashioning that takes root under the form of some imagined possibility for self-cultivation. Consider, for example, the wide range of artistic talents and athletic skills that people cultivate. We are the only kind of vegetation that has some amount of choice over the fruits it produces, the only animal who can self-consciously train itself into becoming what it is not yet. Human temporality thus makes all persons their own midwives. But perhaps obviously, this often includes extending our openness to others, reclaiming the possibilities that have been opened to us because of them. We grow into ourselves, take the task of becoming ourselves in terms of the image we have of ourselves, but this is not solipsism. We can cultivate ourselves according to an image of who we ought to be, and this freedom is our responsibility.

The second horizon refers to all of the ways that our lives bear gifts to others. We transcend the boundaries of our flesh and through our transcendence are able to give to others. Just as my own past was once another's future, so what I call the future is, in its own time, a past for others who are yet to arrive. We, both personally and trans-generationally, both particularly and anonymously, share the boon and the burden of being of the condition of each others' possibilities. We have become who we are because of others, and others become who they are because of us. We are, as Alfred Korzybski stresses, "time-binders," creatures whose existence, unlike other creatures, requires falling into history.

Mediation and transcendence disclose the semipermeable boundaries between self and others, and as we come to understand that there is no "I" independent of other people, we turn our attention to practices of rejuvenating the world.

We come to understand our ambiguous continuities with the rest of the universe as we become open to the metaphysical ambiguity of being both *in* the universe and *of* the universe. What matters is the whole that includes me, not me per se. We discover a life eternal that we, the living, partly are.

But a bit of caution must be expressed, for the more that people focus upon the historical meaning of an individual's life journey, the harder it is to see the cyclical time of many generations. We should not act as if we are simply born atop the shoulders of previous generations, as if cultural progress is simply given to us individually. Although material gains and technologies may be something that culture can bestow and grow in a linear way, cultivation of the spirit is not; at best, spirit can be exemplified, but it is never bestowed by another. There can be no progress other than individual progress in such areas of life. This is precisely Søren Kierkegaard's point where he writes,

> When a breed of sheep, for example, is improved, improved sheep are born because the specimen merely expresses the species. But surely it is different when an individual, who is qualified by spirit, relates himself to the generation….Development of spirit is self-activity; the spiritually developed individual takes his spiritual development along with him in death. If a succeeding individual is to attain it, it must occur through his self-activity. (1992, 345)

Some aspects of our collective and individual lives may be provided by others and may further lead to a sense of cultural progress, but there are many aspects where there is no development without someone's action and will. There are many things that we cannot give directly to others, many ideas, beliefs, competencies, and values we cannot bestow upon them. The best, and perhaps only, thing that we can do is inspire their continuance.

Only persons can embody and maintain resources such as valor, integrity, dignity, duty, honor, courage, tenacity, compassion, forgiveness, faith, respect, and hope. Without actual persons to give these words concrete meaning, they easily become mere slogans or weakly endorsed abstractions, or perhaps, meaningless. How are these virtues carried on if not in the words and deeds, the very lives, of existing individuals? What is the life of each and every one of us, if not a sociohistorical accomplishment that remains *open* for future possibilities?

Finally, humanity is that peculiar part of nature that lives with an image of the eternal, and this horizon of transcendence disregards questions of both death and the world's ongoing state. It focuses only on the ways that the eternal and the perfect are omnipresent dimensions of our lives. It thus seeks no justification for existence outside of the ability to contemplate the eternal and the perfect. Kierkegaard states the matter thusly:

> To exist, one thinks, is nothing much, even less an art...But truly to exist, that is to permeate one's existence with consciousness, simultaneously to be eternal, far beyond it, as it were, and nevertheless present in it and nevertheless in a process of becoming—that is truly difficult. (1992, 308)

If we were but matter, we could be but present. If we were merely animal, we would struggle with both being present and becoming. But to be human is to need a third. Humans must be in the present, nevertheless in the process of becoming, but also practice the art of releasing divinity in the details, of finding horizons of perfection within the mundane duties of everyday life.

It may be that the only way to tolerate one's individuation is to participate joyfully in the self-sacrificial rituals that rejuvenate the world. To heroically give to the world in such a way that more possibility is thereby freed up is to practice that art of giving that helps to liberate what can be said and what can be done. Secular capitalist individualism, within a world of material and technological progress, is a sad hoax, a kind of illness inflicted upon the contemporary literate miser. Persons who mistakenly take themselves as all alone in a wholly visible world and who then cook up a strategy for mere survival within such a mean and low-visioned world-picture, such people have forgotten that they are much older and other than they think they are.

Notes

1   Becker writes, "Money sums up the causa sui project all in itself" (1975, 82). We might add that reliable contraception was, perhaps, an equally powerful force in releasing the modern causa sui project as well.

2   We can find within Burke, especially in his "Epilogue: Prologue in Heaven," the idea that guilt is fundamentally tied to the invention of money (i.e., the symbol of all symbols). Burke suggests that money becomes the symbol for everything, and here we find the relation between Burke and Becker most obvious (cf. Burke 1961, 291-292).

3   Erich Kahler eloquently accounts for the process of natural historical evolution, and he renders the individual as an historical inevitability, one precast by Jesus: "My god, my god, why have you forsaken me?" Whereas for Lacan, the mirror stage is basically a metaphor for natural development, for anthropologist Edmund Carpenter, mirrors and the photographic images played a key historical and cultural role in the emergence of self-reflexive individuation.

4   Admittedly, Burke is quite sophisticated. On the one hand, he expresses his preference for Spinoza's ability to equate God and Nature without reduction to naturalism. Spinoza had retained an active nature, one that had survived many assaults against the charge of teleology. Additionally, at several points Burke refers to human action being partial acts of God's whole act. But on the other hand, Burke comes down hard on Darwin's overstressing of the continuities with animals (cf. 1966). It should be underscored that Burke also does not haggle over the sheer possibility that we are but

bodies in motion. Rather, he maintains that even if action is an illusion, we cannot help but think of ourselves in these terms.

5 "But if mind is prefigured in the organic from the beginning then freedom is." As Jonas continues, "metabolism, the basic level of all organic existence,... is itself the first form of freedom" (1966, 3).

6 Jonas writes,

> Living substance, by some original act of segregation, has taken itself out of the general integration of things in the physical context, set itself over against the world, and introduced the tension of "to be or not to be" into the neutral assuredness of existence....So constitutive for life is the possibility of not-being that its very being is essentially a hovering over this abyss, a skirting on its brink: thus being itself has become a constant possibility rather than a given state, ever anew to be laid hold of in opposition to its ever-present contrary, not-being, which will inevitably engulf it in the end. (1966, 4)

7 Jonas writes, "Life's self-transcendence consists in having a world in which it must reach beyond itself and expand its being within a horizon. This self-transcendence is rooted in an organic need for matter, and this need is based in turn on its formal freedom from matter" (1996, 69).

8 Jonas writes, "Opposing in its internal autonomy the entropy rule of general causality, it is subject to it. Emancipated from the identity with matter, it is yet in need of it... The fear of death with which the hazard of this existence is charged is a never-ending comment on the audacity of the original venture upon which substance embarked in turning organic" (1966, 5).

9 Interested readers should see the works of Bleibtreu, Agamben, Korzybski, Heidegger, and Dennett.

10 Still, locomotion is only a *temporary* possibility, as no animal remains continuously on the move.

11 Cf. Jonas's (1966) chapter "To Move and To Feel."

12 Jonas writes, "The split between subject and object—opened up by perception at a distance and by greater radius of movement, and reflected in the acuteness of appetite and fear, satisfaction and disappointment, enjoyment and pain—was never to be closed again. But in its growing expansion, life's freedom found room for all those ways of relating—perceptive, active and emotional—that justify the split by spanning it and that indirectly regain the lost unity" (1996, 74).

13 By the powers of speech, our perceptions have been transformed into a conceptual order. Speech, the distillation of the logos characterizing the cosmos, opens and extends mediacy on three fronts: outward ranging concern and possible spatial transcendence; backward reaches of historical traditions as well as orientations toward the distant and even final future; and finally, inwardness, meaning levels of self-consciousness found in conversation and reflection. Across all horizons, both persons and the world are conceptualized through increasing degrees both of abstraction and particularization.

14 He states further, "The image becomes detached from the object, that is, the presence of the *eidos* is made independent of that of the thing. Vision involves a stepping back from the importunity of environment and procures the freedom of detached survey" (1966, 170).

15 Jonas writes, "the level of a nonanimal mediacy in the relation to objects, and of a distance from reality entertained and bridged by that mediacy at the same time. The existence of images, which shows form wrested from fact, is a witness to this mediacy, and in its open promise alone suffices as evidence of human freedom" (1966, 174).

16 We cannot answer the question by simply making recourse to the sociohistorical level of analysis. Even if it has been the sum total effect of money and literacy to have released the fully functional anonymous individual, the ontological question remains: why would there by such a possibility? Consider the meaning horizon that Becker brings to this issue: "man is the one animal created by evolution who can use his power for the further liberation of individuals…This liberation would theoretically come about as the disposition over power is made a matter of increasingly responsible individual decision…this is the authentic and basic meaning of the promise of democracy: that it would be the one form of government most in accord with the promise of evolution itself, and that it would seek to turn the paradox of evolution to the fullest development of man's subjectivity" (1969, 112).

17 Could there be something quite revealing in the fact that deep senses of spirituality are often equated with appreciation for *mystery*? This inkling, perhaps, gives us an interpretative thread as to why the eternal ground allowed itself to be divested of its divinity. Only by completely losing itself did mystery begin, and, in turn, mystery then is that experience that humans associate with divinity. Could it be that the mystical sense of awe humans are able to feel in contemplating the ultimate ground of existence is the very mystery that the divine originally sought "in the beginning" (i.e., in the project of losing itself into the unfolding contingencies of action within finitude)?

18 As Jonas further claims:

> If man, as our tale has it, was created "for" the image of God, rather than "in" his image—if our lives become lines in the divine countenance: then our responsibility is not defined in mundane terms alone…Further, as transcendence grows with the terribly ambiguous harvest of deeds, our impact on eternity is for good *and* for evil: we can build and we can destroy, we can heal and we can hurt, we can nourish and we can starve divinity, we can perfect and we can disfigure its image: the scars of one are as enduring as the lustre of the other. (1966, 278)

19 It must be admitted that for Jonas, the universe does not have a "logos" in the ancient sense of the word. He argues explicitly against this position in his *Mortality and Morality*. For his view, God is in peril and cannot rest in the assurance of unfolding according to plan. But the task taken up here is to recover a sense of logos that Burke identifies, and to see that the "final causes" that characterize life are, as Burke suggests, "not futural at all, but a kind of continual present until attainted or abandoned" (1961, 246).

20 Let us imagine an equally horrible fate. The more moral wrongs you do in this world, the more that unknown relatives of yours will be punished and will continue to be punished later. Oh wait, *that is our world!*

21 Some Eastern philosophies suggest that existence is a dance. We, while we dance, do not dance so as to arrive at the end of the dance; the dance is its own reason.

22 As Jonas witnessed the horror of the mid-twentieth century, he also watched many people give up their faith, mostly from their inability to forgive the lack of divine intervention during the Holocaust.

23 Burke offers a contrast for those who think of transcendence in terms of the agent. He suggests that Spinoza "is saying always that we have eternity by reason of our natures as parts of the non-personal *whole* (just as by shifting the stress, we perish by reason of our natures as *parts* of a whole)" (1962, 150).

24 In fact, some Christians so rigorously identify with their inwardness that they are willing to believe that life itself is not a sacred event. Life is merely a test, a kind of cosmic dress rehearsal or prelude for the real show. Arguably, the greatest illusion in human history is that there is a beginning or an ending of the cosmos. This is a pervasive myth that needs to be challenged and revised. We might even attempt to recover the ancient Greek Stoic traditions, which held that the universe endlessly recreates itself and dissolves, but rises to recreate itself again. In this sense, the cosmos has neither a beginning nor ending.

25 Throughout his writings, Becker uses the expression the "life force" as if to identify a teleological drive of mediation. In stressing how all cultures are religious, Becker sought to bring out the spiritual elements of cultural and interpersonal practices, thus bringing together theology, psychology, and natural evolution. In his *Beyond Alienation*, Becker proposes a naturalistic ontology of how life achieves maximum meaning and conviction, and here he discusses theological dimensions that inhere in the simple fact of culture. Becker writes, "The desire of life to keep its identity as a moving feeling force; and yet, at the same time to lose this identity in a peace-giving merger with nature. This paradox is all of a piece with the problem of freedom that we outlined above: how to triumph over the limitations of nature, while yet remaining with nature. ...So we might say that the 'secret' of the greatest possible satisfaction of life is to bring the 'largest amount' of life force into a union with nature" (1967, 174). It is the very success of transcendence that has culminated into the modern causa sui project. But consider too Becker's claims:

> Even the strongest person cannot stand alone, because the finite creature has to get his meanings from outside himself. No, let us even say that especially the strongest person cannot stand alone, because he, above all others, is not bound to any automatically sustained meanings. Nothing holds him or chains him, nothing fetters his view. As a result, he looks about for the largest possible horizon of action and meaning. And when he does, he finds himself alone in the universe itself. In order to keep his action meaningful under this kind of horizon, he must then turn to the object of highest contemplation and meaning—God. God alone can make sense of a free horizon of meaning. Without God, such a horizon is absurd...Man believes either in a God or in an idol; there is no third course open...When life became gradually secular, it became "accidental" instead of divinely necessary; instead of being timeless in its significance, it became historical...It means the anxious fear of unsupported and unsanctioned meanings. (1967, 202-205)

Burke's corpus, as a correlate, examines God as pure Act and takes human action as a limited and partial representation of that Act. Throughout his writings we find Burke expressing his preferences for a Spinozan nature, one that could be divine while not collapsing the divine to nothing but nature. And all three thinkers (Becker, Burke, and Jonas) expressly argue that we, humans, are that part of nature that consciously experiences teleology. Jonas writes,

> It then seems to issue in this choice of monistic alternatives: either to take presence of purposive inwardness in one part of the physical order, viz., in man, as a valid testimony to the nature of that wider reality that lets it emerge, and to accept what it reveals in itself as part of the general evidence; or to extend the prerogatives of mechanical matter to the very heart of the seemingly heterogeneous class of phenomena and oust teleology even from the "nature of man," whence it had tainted the "nature of the universe"—that is, to alienate man from himself and deny genuineness to the self-experience of life. (1966, 37)

"Can we hope to forestall (if it can be forestalled!) the most idiotic tragedy conceivable: the willful ultimate poisoning of this lovely planet, in conformity with a mistaken heroics of war—and each day, as the sun still rises anew upon the still surviving plentitude, let us piously give thanks to Something or Other not of man's making."
(Burke 1985, 5 of the introduction)

*"...back to a life of integral myth,
ritual, fellowship in community...
back to a share in eternal time,
and in eternal tasks...."
(Becker 1967, 214)*

PART II
RECKONING WITH NATURAL GUILT

This book began by examining the contemporary need for self-esteem. I reviewed Ernest Becker's mature trilogy to show how personality and cultural form provide for sustained experiences of self-worth and culminate, somewhat naturally, into styles of heroic death denial. To say as much is to suggest that nature's original causa sui project began with the transcendence of cultural time-binding.[1] We are the location of nature that subjects itself to time-gathering modes of cultural becoming, and moreover, the sociohistorical development of the causa sui project in modern Western cultures came, in due time, to embody nothing less than an attempt to produce individual members who could be the complete cause of themselves and their lives' meanings. Modern Western societies, especially those aligned with secular technological individualism and anonymous consumer-capitalism, became the pervasive attempt to remove or completely hide from the phenomenon of natural guilt.

But natural guilt, chapter 2 attempted to elucidate, is not that easily dispelled, for it is part and parcel of the ambiguities of logos. It is, as Kenneth Burke suggests, a symptom of our being; we endlessly ride upon and yet seem to deny the unending and ambiguous tide of expansion and contraction, merger and division. Guilt emerges because we proceed in action despite our lack of assurance regarding our responsibilities, meaning that we assent to dubious authoritative disambiguations. We are guilty of submission to negative orders of disambiguation that serve partisan interests, at least primarily by the structures that literacy, money, and calendars make possible: property rights, inheritance laws, and accrued compound interest. We also are guilty of various symbolic identifications and disindentifications: racisms, sexisms, and nationalisms. More than anything else, modern Western individuals are guilty of over-exaggerating autonomy and self-sufficiency, and ultimately, of covering over many forms of dependence (natural, social, and technological). But if the ambiguities of logos are the source of natural guilt, and the causa sui project is the natural human response to such ambiguities, then we needed to better understand the nature and origin of logos itself. Accordingly, chapter 3 took up this task.

Looking for the roots of logos chapter 3 came to find them, natural guilt, and the many sociohistorical developments of the causa sui project within a grand cosmological ground, a kind of meta-narrative regarding humans' relations (similarities to and differences from) the rest of the natural world. Drawing mainly upon the philosophical biology of Hans Jonas, I outlined a cosmology where the drive of the causa sui project appears to be precast by modes of transcendence found at various levels in the natural world. At many different phylogenic levels we noted the development of an inward boundary that accomplishes increasing transcendence outward, meaning that the unending dialectic of division (expansion) and merger (contraction) is the forcing-bed of transcendence. We also concluded that, at its fullest culmination, human action bears the cosmic responsibility of rejuvenating and regenerating the world, of recognizing the sacredness of life. We discovered a very real extra-mundane heroism: it is forgiving the cosmos for individuation and celebrating (thus keeping open and available) the many modes of transcendence for others. Significance and/or a meaningful life are therefore most assuredly sought by the self-sacrifice that strives to liberate the transcendence of others, by the self-imposed suffering that is encumbered in cultivating talents, skills, or capacities, and by continuous meditation upon the perfect and the eternal.

The second part of this study integrates the previous three chapters into a general account of the significance of human action and interaction. We finally can understand the real meaning of the contemporary motive of self-esteem: we suffer from cosmic responsibility, a drive for significance or meaning that can only be accomplished or released in an expiative-heroism.

Chapter 4, the first of Part II, draws mainly from the writings of Erving Goffman and explores the ritual elements of social encounters. It reveals worth and value in social interaction as grounded in the recognition of sacredness to life. Its main task is to reinvigorate our contemporary understanding of the need for self-worth and to openly display the logic operating within and beneath everyday conversations. An additional task is to show how consumer capitalism distorts and trivializes the meaning of our need for self-worth and recognition. Chapter 5 turns to the French novelist Antoine de Saint-Exupéry and explores the phenomenon of significance by examining the ritual dimensions of labor. I focus upon "bartering," the self-sacrifice by which we come to "no longer dread death." I also outline a model that could be used to strategically generate the conditions for significance. Chapter 6, the final chapter of this study, develops a neo-Stoic extra-mundane heroism. In broadest form, I attempt to sketch the characteristics of a neo-Stoic cosmopolitanite who most values life's ability to strive toward harmonious order.

Notes

1   In Brown's (1985) sense, culture is the way that the child becomes the parent of the adult.

Man needs a living and daily concern with ultimates, with the mystery of being, and with his role in the perpetuation of being...we understand fully the great world–historical task that has been left to us since the decline of the Greek Stoic ideal...
(Becker 1967, 220)

*"Life is essentially relationship;
and relation as such implies 'transcendence,'
a going-beyond-itself on the part
of that which entertains the relation."*
(Jonas 1966, 5)

CHAPTER 4

RITUAL ELEMENTS OF FACE-TO-FACE ENCOUNTERS

Life is sacred and humanity is the location of life where sacredness becomes self-conscious. If you want to see this sacredness close up, under glass as it were, simply take a good look at face-to-face interaction. Intercourse between self-conscious beings requires ritual, for ritual is that horizon of experience whereby sacredness receives proper handling and ceremonial care. Of all the different kinds of beings in the world, humans are the most aware of how they are treated, understood, and esteemed. But we are not merely the largest of peacocks; our boasts and displays can occur within grand contexts, situations whose boundaries are not readily seen and may even be given to unseen audiences. They thereby unfold as gifts of sacrifice, heroic offerings presented with grateful acknowledgment of dependence upon a sacred mystery that unifies life and that requires renewal and regeneration.

This chapter, accordingly, explores the ritual practices that ensconce and laminate face-to-face interaction. It examines the ways that we manage and sanctify the worth and value of humans and their dealings, the ways that we protect them from contamination. I here draw heavily upon the writings of Erving Goffman, taking his orientation to ritual to provide great insight regarding the heroic-expiative significance nestled within interpersonal interaction. Unfortunately, a good deal of contemporary characterizations of Goffman's ideas either criticize the triviality and vanity of self-performance in modern culture, or they reduce his discussions of self/face/ritual to a kind of functionality or instrumentality: ritual is flatly reduced to "routine" or is treated as mere "social lubricant." What these kinds of criticism and/or appropriations have fundamentally misunderstood is the underlying logic of ritual practices: *sacrament*. Characterizing this trend as well as coming to Goffman's defense, Becker nicely sets the frame for my continued discussion. I quote him at length:

> Many people have scoffed at Goffman's delineation of the everyday modern rituals of face-work and status forcing; they argued that these types of

petty self-promotion might be true of modern organization men hopelessly set adrift in bureaucratic society but these kinds of shallow one-upmanship behaviors couldn't possibly be true of man everywhere...I have noted elsewhere that I think these critics of Goffman are very wrong, and I repeat it here because it is more in context with the deeper understanding of primitive society...It is only in modern society that the mutual imparting of self-importance has trickled down to the simple maneuvering of face-work; there is hardly any other way to get a sense of value except from the boss, the company dinner, or the random social encounter in the elevator or on the way to the executive toilet. It is pretty demeaning—but that is not Goffman's fault, it is the playing out of the historical decadence of ritual. Primitive society was a formal organization for the apotheosis of man. Our own everyday rituals seem shallow precisely because they lack the cosmic connection...I think it is safe to say that primitive organization for ritual is the paradigm and ancestor to all face-work, and that archaic ritual is nothing other than in-depth face-work. (Becker 1975, 15-16)

Taking Becker's defense of Goffman as my point of departure, I explore the possibility of recovering the experience of "in-depth face-work." The spirit that calls for recognition is not some kind of petty and self-serving, "Oh how important and wonderful am I. Look at me. I'm so special." On the contrary, to grasp the need for self-worth it is best to acknowledge that prior to any self-regard is the experience of the overwhelming awesomeness of the cosmos. In the face of such powerful and all-encompassing magnificence, and because we are dumbfounded regarding the origins of all life including our own, we are stricken with the question: How do I "relate" to what is obviously powerful, awesome, and transcending? Only by first being mesmerized and baffled at the world's absolute wonderfulness does the problem of "self-worth" come into focus.

Another part of the challenge is to grant that all of life is sacred without flattening or leveling the world into a plane where all is at equal value. Hierarchy and orders of rank, which imply differing statuses and stratified claims to publicly recognized esteem, will always characterize societies everywhere. The task at hand, then, will be to reveal the sense of sacredness disentangled from modern "canons of pecuniary prowess" (cf. Veblen 1899) and from other fortunes of happenstance and luck, from all of that which is naturally beyond an individual's control. From this perspective, we must learn how to recognize the legitimate claim to worth and value—*even the experience of comparative worth*—without relying upon some measure of monetary superiority or deference to office status and bureaucratic position. The critical question is: what are legitimate grounds for comparative senses of worth and value? More on this throughout, but for now I offer: self-discipline, courage, generosity, moderation, forbearance, prudence, and discretion as some basic criteria for differential veneration. Are these not less dubious than wealth, sex, age, race, and/or occupation?

In order to show the heroic and expiative dimensions that Becker sought to identify, recover, and develop, I turn to the nettlesome density of everyday face-to-face interaction. I try to reveal a basic logic throughout face-to-face ritual practices and to show a repressed and degenerated horizon of meaning, one that remains open for resuscitation. First, though, I begin by reviewing some obstacles that must be put into perspective, obstacles that hide from view the heroic and expiative underbelly to face-to-face interaction.

Clearing the Path

A good way to begin, perhaps, is to suggest that meaning is possible only where there is propriety and that propriety is possible only where there is order. This is true at all levels of meaning, meaning that meaning is inseparable from the sense of order. Where anyone at anytime can equally say or do anything to anyone else with equal effect, the conditions have been set for utter meaninglessness.

Human life, to the degree that it is meaningful, requires modes of merger and division, ritual actions and practices that orient themselves according to existential particulars (cf. Anton 2008). Such particulars are evident in that people are not simply interchangeable; they have shared or unshared pasts, occupy different places in various social hierarchies, participate in kinds of identifications, and share or not in interpretations of relation-states. This non-interchangeability of persons leads Goffman to admonish: "In face-to-face talk the social and personal identity of the listeners will oblige the speakers to preselect on the basis of a whole range of fundamental factors—propriety being at issue, not merely disambiguation" (1981, 255). What is appropriate or called for by one person is inappropriate, even a violation, if performed by the wrong person. This fundamental non-interchangeability of persons can be illustrated if we comparatively consider some levels of meaning where ritual dimensions seem irrelevant or momentarily suspended.

Students of language and linguistics often find it useful to distinguish at least three kinds of meaning in verbal utterance (cf. Olson 1994). The first is known as semantic meaning. Semantic meaning deals with the issue of reference and often is addressed in term of single words, with the *referent* of a word being its "meaning." In semiotic theory and linguistics, the issue of semantics is discussed as selections and substitutions within the "vertical axis." Questions of semantics can sometimes be settled by recourse to pointing or the dictionary, though certainly some words are better grasped in Burke's terms as "personal equations," some even being, as George Steiner would say, "semantically private." At any rate, one layer of meaning is semantic meaning.

In addition to semantic meaning is syntactical meaning. Syntax is a higher order of meaning, dealing with combinations of relationships, temporal tenses, and modes of word agreement. Literacy scholar David Olson nicely makes evident the nature of syntactical meaning where he compares the phrases "a Venetian blind" and "a blind Venetian." Here we find a kind of meaning that is accomplished by the combination and ordering of the words, not the words themselves. Syntax is also vital to analysis because it allows us to isolate and discuss a substance's constituent elements. By use of the word "is," for example, we can analytically parcel out essential and accidental properties (the ball is round, the cup is blue). In semiotic theory and linguistics, the issue of syntactical meaning is discussed in terms of combinations along the "horizontal axis."

The third layer of meaning is pragmatics, and it refers to a still higher order of meaning: the sense of "audience-directed intention." When we want to know not what an utterance means but what the speaker means by the utterance, we are asking about pragmatic meaning. A great deal of such meaning is conveyed para-linguistically and by extra-verbal cues. Pragmatic meaning is often called the "illocutionary force" of an utterance, with the propositional content (some combination of semantic and syntactical meaning) called the "locutionary act." Most generally, the study of pragmatics turns to the varieties of "speech genres" beyond the mere conveyance of propositional content: hints, jokes, sarcastic remarks.

Now, in addition to the three layers of meaning already mentioned, consider a fourth layer: ritual meaning. Ritual meaning refers to the moment-by-moment experience of character, one's own and/or another's, as accomplished in either harmony or dissonance with situational propriety.[1] Ritual meaning, in contrast to the above three kinds of meaning, is not an issue of disambiguation regarding semantic, syntactic, nor pragmatic meaning. It does not simply align with what Goffman (1981, 22-29) has called "system constraints," meaning the kinds of constraints that boil down to semantics, syntactics, and/ or pragmatics. Ritual surpasses the realm of functionality and offers a clue to the underlying sacredness to humans and their dealings. We have, then, four kinds of meaning in verbal face-to-face interaction:

Semantic= Relations of words to their referents
Syntactic= Relations of word combination and word order
Pragmatic= Speaker's attitude toward own words/ audience-directed
                intention
Ritualistic= Felt alignment to sacred orders and propriety

The ritualistic elements in conversational encounters refer to the *conduct* of particular persons on particular occasions, and ritual meaning, therefore, shows itself as an embodied texture where character is experienced and handled. Goffman provides an eloquent summary of these background issues as well as gives a succinct prelude to the ideas needing further address:

> Instead, then, of merely an arbitrary period during which the exchange of messages occurs, we have a social encounter, a coming together that ritually regularizes the risks and opportunities face-to-face talk provides, enforcing the standards of modesty regarding self and considerateness for others generally enjoined in the community. (1981, 19)

The task at hand is to unpack several different kinds of ritualistic meaning, and all along demonstrate how propriety accords with existential particularity. This further means that many practices of ceremonial care (rituals of division and merger) laminate spoken interaction, and the flow of the conversation is regulated, both in content and in performance, according to who, particularly, is involved.

The Nature of Ritual Meaning

The ritual meaning within conversational encounters can be clarified by first offering a more precise definition of the word "ritual." Ritual, Goffman suggests, refers to an "act through which an individual portrays his respect and regard for some object of ultimate value to that object of ultimate value or to its stand-in" (1971, 62). In face-to-face conversation, ritual refers to the texture and fabric by which persons appropriately handle themselves and other people. If they are not to be violated, people must be treated with some degree of adequate ceremony, with propriety mainly emerging from particularity and a sense of sacred, hierarchic mystery.

In organization, form, and contour, ritual practices depend upon various acts of merger and division that preserve sacramental substances from contamination. Sensing that particular others, events, or objects will be contaminating (and that particular others will deem us to be a contaminant), we not only commonly avoid certain people, places, and things, but, throughout everyday dealings, we find many "brief rituals one individual performs for and to another, attesting to civility and good will on the performer's part and to the recipient's possession of a small patrimony of sacredness" (Goffman 1971, 63). Without such ritual practices, I am suggesting, there is insufficient texture or inadequate room for the experience of character.

When someone is experienced as being sincere, honorable, dignified, tactful, witty, intelligent, rude, ostentatious, deceitful, or incompetent, it is only in accordance with ritual practices that these substances or qualities can be actually *experienced*. Goffman writes,

> To be a given kind of person, then, is not merely to possess the required attributes, but also to sustain the standards of conduct and appearance that one's social grouping attaches thereto…A status, a position, a social place is not a material thing to be possessed and then displayed; it is a pattern of appropriate conduct, coherent, embellished, and well articulated. (Goffman 1959, 75)

The experience of character, *one's own or another's*, is concretely articulated within conversational encounters according to manners of complying with or forgoing various ritual traditions. In giving and claiming worth and value, or perhaps demeaning or desecrating, rituals give dramatic light to existence.[2] This general point can be clarified further by first walking through two main kinds of ritual and by demonstrating how their specific sense of propriety is articulated by existential particulars that fall, roughly, into the following three groupings: the "occasion," the "current relation states," and "externally-based attributes."

Properly Tending the Sacred

In discussing ritual types, Goffman (1971) appropriates Durkheim's distinction between positive and negative ritual. Recalling this distinction: positive ritual consists in various small offerings that are felt to be mutually obligated when persons gather together for a momentary encounter or a sustained interaction. The general spirit of positive ritual is to convey by ceremony a sense of worth and value. Negative ritual, on the other hand, consists in the felt sense of obligation to grant distance and to have territorial claims unimpeded. The general spirit of negative ritual is to give proper avoidance and to prevent any acts of contamination.

Negative Ritual

Negative ritual basically emerges as a symptom; it comes from the felt sense of sacredness. It is, therefore, not surprising to find conversational barriers and many implicitly held expectations that ritually organize when and where who talks to whom and about what. By simple maintenance of appropriate distance—many acts of avoidance and symbolically keeping away—negative ritual practices protect persons from being asked embarrassing questions or questions designed to expose flaws in moral character. They also protect people from the embarrassment of contaminating others. In general, as Goffman suggests, much can be gained by venturing little.

Negative ritual organizes the form and flow of spoken encounters to a degree that is difficult to overstate, though a persistent challenge to revealing negative ritual is that it easily eludes direct observation. Practiced through avoidance, a kind of "division-from," negative ritual is always a "merger-with" something or someone else. Burke hits on this issue where he writes about monastic practices informed by adherence to various "thou-shalt-nots" and how "the day may be filled with a constant succession of positive acts. Yet they are ultimately guided or regulated by proscriptive principles, involving acquiescence to vows consciously and conscientiously taken" (1966, 11). This means that countless negative rituals are performed but they are overlooked as acts in their own right. As people practice avoidance of those places, people, or topics where their welcome wears thin, they are nevertheless obligated to be somewhere doing something. Let me clarify further with a range of examples.

Gaze, eye directedness, and intention display, these are not merely part of a natural or objective process known as "seeing." To look is to be someone; it is to take a position as someone who understands where to look and where not to look. Men in bars can provoke fights if someone looks the wrong way at somebody or if someone is staring too long at another person. The property of eye gaze is also evident in public bathroom behavior. Men stand facing the urinal and they look at the wall, the ceiling, straight down, that is, at anything but some other guy's privates. In cross-sex conversation, males and females do not spend the entire time staring into each other's eyes; gaze moves around a little. A commonly known example is of a young male who is caught staring at a woman's breasts/body. In such cases, the woman may feel devalued and may take the man to be a "letch" or a "creep." Indeed, how much of our sense of character (both our own and others') comes from gaze and eye comportment?

On many occasions and in many public places, individuals avoid initiating spoken exchanges with others with whom they are unacquainted, particularly if those others are already accompanied or are of a different social class or status. This simple and routine kind of avoidance is a prime example of negative ritual. Hence, to avoid an unwanted request for engagement, particularly from a stranger, someone may strategically avoid any eye contact while projecting purposeful looks elsewhere. Note though, using such a strategy on certain occasions, or to particular acquaintances, could result in a demerit to one's own character, or an insult to the other's.

Although any individual may be physically available to all others at a given occasion or public place, individuals are ritually accessible to a much lesser degree, and this applies on a variety of levels. First, persons who are not sanctified as participants in a conversation, that is "onlookers," will be expected to display

what Goffman (1963a, 156) aptly calls "civil inattention." Unacquainted bystand-
ers may even ritualize the act of not eavesdropping; they give a small show of
being sustained and maintained in other involvements, or at the least, overt demonstrations of being inattentive to messages being shared. Second, as a dialogic
complement, those in the conversation are neither to challenge the onlookers'
displays by bellowing tales so sensational and lurid that onlookers will be unable
to disattend, nor to insult the integrity of the onlookers' displays by huddling or
whispering too furtively. Should such secretive cover be required for information
exchange, people routinely employ an "involvement shield," such as a bathroom
or other private area, so as to avoid overly taxing ritual demands. These twin
aspects of negative ritual sanctify and confirm an "existential particularity" to
face-to-face conversation. And the logic is clear: Availability of various types
of information is perpetually oscillating between concealment and disclosure—
between inclusion and exclusion—depending upon the location, occasion, and
who, particularly, is involved.

In addition to the dividing practices that keep unacquainted people from
being forced into encounters with each other, there are many negative ritual practices that are best described as "partitioning practices." Goffman presents a host
of terms and concepts such as "talk lines,"[3] "fugitive signs,"[4] "collusion,"[5] and
"evidential boundaries,"[6] all which recognize that information is ritually parti-
tioned off so that the experience of character emerges in conjunction with who is
"in the know" as well as who, specifically, is "kept in the dark." Notions of "pri-
vacy" and "confidentiality" are perhaps the clearest and most direct illustrations
of the meaning of negative ritual. For example, medical community practitioners
not only have to deal with various kinds of confidential information, but they
also work with people who, not wanting to be embarrassed or compromised in
their self-image, do not report honestly about their lifestyle practices and health
behaviors.

For my final consideration of negative ritual, I turn to the special partitioning practice of conversational avoidance. Most obviously, individuals routinely
avoid particular others. Less obvious, conversations are regulated in topics and
tones according to who is *not* present in person. Goffman discusses the "Treatment of the Absent" and rightfully notes that "there are very few friendship relationships in which there is not some occasion when attitudes expressed about the
friend behind his back are grossly incompatible with the ones expressed about
him to his face" (1959, 170). Children are routinely taught that it is impolite to
talk about others behind their backs, and yet this is a regular ritual practice of everyday life. But we must add that not all talk behind another's back is derogatory
or condemning. There are also acts of social modesty where we do not lavishly

praise others to their faces. In a word, the absent are just as likely to be talked about with complimentary and overly-boasted praises as they are to be discredited and damned. Moreover, the point to be underscored here is that regardless of whether such talk is praising or condemning, the logic of negative ritual depends upon the basic non-interchangeability of interactants. It is particularity that sets the conditions for the negative rituals that then accomplish and sustain the sense of character. Said more simply, during face-to-face interaction, the topics, tones, and sheer coming together of individuals are all ritually regulated by who, *particularly*, is engaged. I return to the importance of non-interchangeability where I discuss positive ritual, but for present purposes, simply note that modesty and tact become possible only as people speak differently, if not in content then at least in tone, according to a particular person's presence or absence. Such observances express regard for character and "face," and additionally, they implicate a ceremonial expression to the current relation statuses, relations not only to the absent, but to those with whom someone talks.

I have discussed how negative ritual is based on the principle of avoidance and how it serves to keep separate those who could contaminate or who would be contaminated. Given the underlying notion that the human self is sacred and must be treated with ceremonial care, the fact that people routinely observe such ritual distance should not be surprising. But what happens when avoidance is neither avoidable nor even desirable? Here we come upon the many practices of positive ritual.

Positive Ritual

Whereas negative ritual keeps separate those of foul or non-relation, (or keeps certain people away from certain occasions as well as from certain others and their informational preserves), "positive ritual" generally refers to the many little offerings of various kinds through which we give and receive esteem and veneration. Everyday conversation is shot through with ritualized expressions of worth, such expressions being conveyed subtly and mostly unthinkingly through tonal accent, vocalic intonations, bodily deportment, facial expressions, and eye inclusiveness, among others. Through this "body idiom"[7] we not only accent and clarify messages (i.e., offer assistance in interpreting illocutionary force), we ritually negotiate and experience character, both others' and our own.

"Positive ritual," Goffman tells us, "tends to be restricted to individuals in a personal relationship" (1971, 91). This means that positive ritual is mainly performed between and among personal acquaintances.[8] But this is not wholly the case, for one of the main forms of positive ritual is the sheer act of grooming and appropriate self-presentation. Also included are all of those elements of politeness and probity that laminate and overfill the traffic wending of the unacquainted as they move through public space. Although these acts are clear illustrations of positive ritual, we can better grasp the underlying logic if we attend, as Goffman suggests, to those ritual performances that come into play as the already acquainted gather and sustain states of mutual involvement.

Two obvious sub-domains of positive ritual are "access rituals,"[9] popularly known as greetings and farewells. It must be underscored that greetings are not like the fax whistle or Internet connection sound that establishes that communication lines are cleared for transmissions; it is not simply a report, a "directional signal"[10] that is to communicate that one is currently available to the other for message exchanges. Granted that greetings include this function, they always involve a paying of some kind of ritual due. For example, arriving to an occasion, people commonly give some kind of greeting to acquaintances, displaying both subtle and dramatic shows of appreciated value for the other and self as well as signifying the current relation states with that particular other. Vocal expressiveness, eye inclusiveness, facial expressions, embraces, and forms of physical contact (e.g., handshake, kiss on the hand or cheek, pat on the back), all of these are necessary for the experience of character. Consider a simple example: Walking through a public space, we are approached by a group of four—one is an old friend not seen for a long time, another is a someone we recently met but do not know well, the third is a stranger, and the fourth is a person who has been a longstanding nemesis (e.g., a soured relationship or some kind of anti-friend). Upon such an encounter, we would likely express, without too much thought about it, a different greeting to each person. For the first, an embrace could be involved, whereas for the last, a civil nod of acknowledgment might be all that is given. We do not greet everyone we meet with the same amount of pomp and circumstance. We ritually perform, in some way or other, how intimate and close the relationship is and how we value the present encounter with this particular other. And greetings are also ceremonially attenuated to display the amount of time between the last or until the next face-to-face engagement. Most generally depicted, contact with others calls for payment of appropriate ritual dues, and failure to pay can precipitate an embarrassment or insult, perhaps giving grounds for questioning the character or present situation of the would-be offender.

Additional grasp of the relationship between the experiences of character and positive ritual practices can be found, as already suggested, in farewells. Imagine that you are talking to someone and the person, while you are midsentence, simply turns and walks away without saying a word. Such a "direct cut" would likely result in insult or indignation and a questioning of the character of the now departed. In contrast to such cuts, farewells often delay and prolong the departure so as to convey worth and value. We may even "act interested" when we are not, for we sometimes neither want to be seen as rude and disrespectful nor do we wish to insult or devalue our interlocutor. And, dialogically, farewells are sometimes ritually expedited, as a show of respect and deference by not taxing the other's willingness to attend to us. Farewells are, therefore, shows of both polite self-presentation and demonstrations of appreciation for the other person and the relationship.[11]

Character is experienced in accordance with positive ritual, and this fact becomes highly evident as we attend to "remedial exchanges,"[12] rituals that correct or give appropriate remedy to minor and major "incidents." Our everyday lives brim with many, if ever so tiny, employments of "accounts," "apologies," "explanations," "minimizations," and all kinds of "tactful blindness." Without such a ritual tapestry of politeness, we would be unable to offer remedy to symbolic offenses to an occasion, to others, or to distance ourselves from unwanted characterizations. When people fumble, spill things on themselves or others, misspeak, or in any other way "fall out of order," some kind of ritual remedy comes into play. For example, if someone tips over a gravy boat during dinner and then says "Who put that there?," we find a different ritual element of character than if someone were to quickly apologize and offer to clean it up. To the former, unless it is the Queen of Sheba, we are likely to be insulted and to take the offender as crass and arrogant in addition to being a klutz. To the latter, we might try to help the situation by further minimization of the incident. We might say, "don't worry about it, could have happened to anyone." We might even tell the story of the really big gravy spill at the 1985 Thanksgiving Day family reunion. At any rate, the actual offender may be the preferred one to make amends (thereby demonstrating knowledge of, and proper respect for, ritual order), but positive rituals admittedly do take a cooperative effort. Goffman thus summarizes the dialogical orientation underlying most positive ritual, where he maintains that the "combined rule of self-respect and the rule of considerateness is that a person tends to conduct himself during an encounter so as to maintain both his own face and the face of the other participants" (1967, 11).

Relevant here is that face-work is routinely performed in response to verbal blunders and linguistic mistakes as well as to statements that inadvertently offend. This fact makes apparent that the linguistic competencies discussed earlier (semantic, syntactic, and pragmatic) cannot be wholly separated from ritual dimensions. In fact, we find that attention to word choice and sentence construction may be highly beneficial, for the question of someone's character is sometimes based on that person's ability to speak articulately or with presence of mind. Moreover, a speaker's perspicuity may not only reveal character attributes such as being erudite or dignified (or perhaps conceited), but may pay a high regard to listeners by thereby acknowledging them as worthy and competent interlocutors.

The underlying nature of positive ritual, as ceremonies of worth and value, can be gasped by attending to our experiences of *love* and *veneration*. When we have great degrees of affection, admiration, and/or respect for people and are in a conversation with them, we may be more attentive to the positive ritual elements of the interaction. But it is not only in love and veneration that we directly feel the sway of positive ritual practices. Two general levels would need to be admitted: first and foremost, all humans, as embodiments of life, are worthy of care and respect. There is a basic minimum respect to which all life should be granted. Second, there is a level of worth and value that is unevenly distributed across and between people, the most primitive or "natural" is that of shared history and of having grown together in some way. People can grow to love those who they know well and such love can become the basis for differential valuation.

In today's society, where a substantial amount of interaction with others is grounded in kinds of functional individual anonymity (shrouded in literacy and money), individuals are unable to draw upon known personal histories or shared past experiences. Too commonly, claims to worth and value are made by demonstrating wealth or affluence. But there are other standards that meet our senses of value: Not only can individuals be esteemed for the personal virtues they have cultivated (justice, courage, moderation, and prudence), but there are many interpersonal virtues such as graciousness, modesty, and goodwill.

For my final consideration of positive ritual, I address how ritual bears upon the selection of topics of discussion. Not only do we use different tones and levels of visual inclusiveness for different people, not only do we speak to certain people in certain ways, but one of the central difficulties to be met in social occasions is furnishing what Goffman has called, "safe supplies."[13] Such supplies are topics of conversations that neither openly discredit present others nor do they pry into private informational territories. Surveying many etiquette manuals, Goffman concludes that in polite society "'open' topics of conversation may thus be maintained in preparation for newcomers. A conversation that by its tone forbade the entrance of new members would be improper" (Goffman 1963a, 173). Messages spoken during a public occasion should not directly offend anyone's rights or competencies as a worthy individual and should provide an appropriate and engaging involvement for ratified participants. Goffman well sums the general spirit of this ritual practice:

> These two tendencies, that of the speaker to scale down his expressions and
> that of the listeners to scale up their interests, each in the light of the other's

capacities and demands, form the bridge that people build to one another, allowing them to meet for a moment of talk in a communion of reciprocally sustained involvement. (1967, 116)

As an additional illustration, we can note that people commonly employ verbal hedges, qualifiers, and commitment restrictions not simply in an attempt to lend precision to an argument, but to lessen the offense to others' faces should their views significantly differ as well as lessen the risk to the speaker's character by giving some qualified distance from any controversial positions advanced.

The non-interchangeability of individual persons often extends into topical or subject matter, especially when the actual topic or subject matter is a mutual acquaintance. With regard to talking about others or about oneself, modesty rules and privilege rules must be observed. There is a certain positive ritual demand, similar to the special treatment given to the absent, which refers to the interplay of who can say what about whom to whom when all are present. On some occasions, ritual propriety suggests that a person does not "convey about himself what others are ready to convey about him to him…the individual must rely on others to complete the picture of him of which he himself is allowed to point only certain parts" (Goffman 1967, 84). In some cases, perhaps in most, improprieties (and awkward feelings of character) occur simply because of who said what to whom, or simply because of who heard what was said by whom.[14]

Negative Ritual = proper avoidance	Positive Ritual = ceremonies of worth
Gaze	Grooming
No staring	Politeness
Civil inattention	Cooperative face-work
Involvement shield	Access rituals (greetings/farewells)
Audience segregation	Corrective interchange
-Treatment of the Absent	

Figure 4.1. Some basic kinds of negative and positive ritual

I can summarize both negative and positive ritual by saying that wherever we find ritual, we also find a sense of sacredness, one that calls for propriety and order. In practice, this means that we avoid those others, those topics of conversation, and those occasions where we fear contamination of either self and/or others. On other occasions, when we do come into face-to-face contact with others, our experience of their character as well as our own is felt in accordance with various ritual ceremonies of worth and value.

Three Lines of Ritual Regard

I have argued that the sense of interpersonal propriety takes its form from the felt sense of sacredness, a sacredness that we attend to and manage by both negative and positive ritual practices. The task remaining is to show how propriety regarding ritual practices is articulated according to three lines of ritual regard: "*occasion*," "*current relation-states*," and "*externally-based attributes*." These three lines of ritual regard are inseparable from the amount of negative ritual and the amount of positive ritual that are felt to be proper or appropriate. They are key factors that bear on the degree to which avoidance is felt to be proper and the extent to which veneration seems to be appropriate. The *proper* amount of negative ritual and the *proper* amount of positive ritual are calibrated according to the occasion, current relation-states, as well as an individual's externally-based attributes. Take, for example, the character attributes of being polite, nice, thoughtless, crass, rude, "cool," generous, poised, witty, brazen, heartless, cold, callous, or kind, among others. Our actual experiences of these attributes (in ourselves and/or in others) are inseparable from the organization of propriety in interaction. Most generally stated, when actions fall into alignment with the ritual order, we experience favorable or desirable dimensions of character, whereas actions out of alignment with ritual propriety lead us to experience unfavorable or undesirable dimensions of character.

The three lines of ritual regard can be briefly previewed by suggesting the following: "*Regard for the Occasion*" spans the fullest possible range of both positive and negative ritual practices on particular occasions, including festival celebrations, funerals, weddings, births, birthdays, routine modern "workdays," informal "get-togethers," and all sorts of mundane encounters. "*Regard for Current Relation-States*" includes those positive and negative rituals that are a calibration according to relation-states such as: relative, loved one, co-worker, friend, neighbor, stranger, boss, ex-friend, ex-lover, hostile enemy. "*Regard for Externally-Based Attributes*" refers to all those positive and negative rituals that align to items external to a particular occasion and/or the current relationship; these span age, sex, race, occupation, economic status, celebrity, known talents or competencies. We should note that the third line of regard became more and more dominant in Western history, especially as modern cities and urban development increasingly facilitated the functional interaction of anonymous individuals. This line of regard is also most subject to valuations and assessments according to pecuniary prowess and invidious comparison (cf. Veblen 1899).

In the modern Western world, these three lines of ritual regard overlap, intersect, and interact. And, even if in the thicket of concrete interactions they intertwine and remain ambiguous implicates of each other, they often enough do congeal to make various kinds of ritual practices appropriate while making others inappropriate. By watching the interplay between the lines of regard and the kinds of rituals and their degree of attenuation, we can outline basic resources for imparting and sanctifying value and for cultivating character in concrete interaction.

The Occasion

People routinely give "appropriate"[15] regard for the situation and/or properly enact respect for the occasion of an encounter. If we look back at figure 4.1, we find that both positive and negative rituals vary according to the occasion. This means that any occasion holds a sense of ritual order, and this order is felt in varying degrees and is managed by positive and negative ritual practices. So, a funeral is not a wedding; a classroom lecture is not a family reunion. A neighborhood backyard barbeque is neither a candlelight dinner for two nor a locker room shower. Each occasion calls for a level/mode of grooming, a level of self-presentation, and an assumed amount of personal involvement or dis-attendance. Depending upon one's current relation-states and externally-based attributes, different kinds of self-presentation seem to be appropriate. In simplest terms: sex, age, and occupation often bear upon what is felt to be appropriate attire for any occasion, though relation-states also have some bearing.

Occasions can be usefully broken down into main involvement and side involvement, and here two interrelated issues must be addressed: First is the amount of focused attention that needs to be given to the main involvement, and second is the amount of allowance given for side involvements. Any occasion, said quite otherwise, will vary in how those two issues are felt to be appropriate. There will be some engagements where practices of avoidance are maintained, others where interaction is encouraged. Street corners and alleyways are not normally the preferred venue for meeting new people. Bars, especially if one sits alone, somewhat invite others to make overtures for interaction. In such situations, tact, modesty, dignity, poise, as well as awkwardness and foolishness accord to how actions align, or do not, with the prevailing occasion.

A final and related consideration of occasion is what is known as "ethos." Goffman, drawing from Bateson, explains ethos by suggesting that occasions commonly assume—and hence come to be ordered by—a certain spirit (e.g., seriousness, jocularity, lugubriousness) that can embody moment-to-moment drifts, especially among smaller circles within a larger occasion (cf. 1963a, 97). Such drifts imply that what is well received during one moment can be received with an awkward distancing silence at another. We can imagine a funeral where a certain joke, said by the right person at the right time, might well be the epitome of social grace and may help to provide a momentary respite from sorrow. But, on the other hand, a different joke, or one said by someone else, or even the same one said at a slightly different moment, would be inappropriate and may embarrass some, anger others, and cause feelings of shame or social inadequacy in the offender. Ethos can be witnessed also in the ebb and flow of classroom discussions. There are moments when someone can appropriately blurt out a comment or statement, while there are other times where such outbursts are largely unacceptable.

In sum of how occasion bears upon felt ritual propriety, people commonly display an alignment with the prevailing mood of an encounter, which also carries the demand that contradictory or personal feelings be held in abeyance. As Goffman suggests, "Through the ceremonial order that is maintained by a system of etiquette, the capacity of the individual to be carried away by a talk becomes socialized, taking on a burden of ritual value and social function" (1967, 115). Individuals are expected to allocate a proper amount of attention to the occasion's main involvements, and thus, people can sometimes give the outward appearance of being spontaneously involved even when they are disinterested.[16] Given the expectation that an individual's comportments be within the spirit of the occasion, it is not surprising that some persons, those who anticipate an inability to adequately meet these constraints, will tactfully avoid the occasion altogether. Such a rejection is likely to be less offensive than would be an unsustainable show of appreciation within the encounter.

Current Relation-States

Face-to-face exchanges naturally exude displays of regard to particular individuals, and the sense of appropriate regard depends not only upon the occasion, but also upon current relation-states. A self, as Goffman suggests, is expected to be "not merely a mechanical relay but someone to whom a relationship of sorts must be extended and expressively confirmed" (1974, 473). This means that individuals commonly overlay their verbal messages with a gloss that expresses appropriate regard to those others with whom they are comingling. They offer appreciation for the other and for currently enjoyed relation-states. Hence, communicative acts, because of a felt sense of ritual order, can be intrusive or imposing when performed by one individual, and yet, the same acts may be perfectly appropriate when performed by someone else. Whereas parents may wipe clean the faces of their children, they cannot wipe clean a stranger's face. The acts that are appropriate (for some people) on a first date are different than those that might be appropriate one year into a relationship, as they would be different after a "breakup."

People experience a sense of propriety or ritual order as articulated by current relation-states. But what, the reader may ask, is "ritual order" or "ceremonial propriety"? Clearly, the order I have been considering here is not physical or even a logical system that inevitably must be followed. Someone could breach the demands of just about any ritual constraint mentioned in this chapter. For example, people do not normally, even if they could, initiate an encounter with a stranger by disclosing dark and self-discrediting secrets; people could, though most do not, use Thanksgiving Day dinner as a chance to articulately disclose in good detail their latest—and coincidentally their best—sexual performances. Even though we are physically capable of proclaiming, "I love you" to random passersby on street corners, most of us do not do such things.[17] These acts, as improprieties to different ceremonial demands, reveal a basic freedom to do so. Hence, although people are ultimately free to break any and every sense of ritual propriety, they are not free from the judgments and meaningful appraisals others could (and probably will) make about their regard for the occasion, for others, if not their moral character.

Our verbal exchanges in most of our everyday encounters are not simply "to whom it may concern messages." We speak to particular others and in particular ways. This non-interchangeability of persons and the importance of attending to particular relation-states lead Goffman to admonish that

> the very forms of behavior employed to celebrate and affirm relationships—rituals such as greetings, enquiries after health, and love-making—are very close in character to what would be a violation of preserves if performed between wrongly related individuals. (1971, 58)

Thus, ritual practices, both positive and negative, have particularity as their basis for distinguishing ritually appropriate responses and interactions from inappropriate ones. There seems a "tacit assumption, an assumption carefully preserved, that what the audience hears was formatted just for them and for this occasion" (Goffman 1981, 188), and this is partly why prepared "pickup lines" can make people appear tacky and shallow.

In sum, current relation-states between interlocutors specify the appropriateness of where and when who is likely to say what to whom. By compliance with—or neglect of—these ceremonial observances, individuals provide displays of regard or disregard for the occasion, for the particular others, and/or for self. Given a pervasive sense that messages ought to be appropriate to the relation status as well as to the occasion, many messages are withheld simply because of the particular relationships of those involved (e.g., in-laws, superiors, bosses, anti-friends). It is, moreover, this fact of non-interchangeability that explains why a person "seems to have a special license to accept mistreatment at his own hands that he does not have the right to accept from others" (Goffman 1967, 32). The relation of the speaker to what was said as well as to whom it was said and where it was said, all of these are part of the felt sense of ritual order.

Externally-Based Attributes

The third and final line of regard pertains to "externally-based attributes."[18] In public, and on certain occasions, individuals not only give ceremonial regard to the occasion and to the particular others who are co-present, they also give ritual expressions of self-esteem and make subtle claims to self-worth based at attributes that are external to the occasion. People "give" and "give off" expressions that can be taken as statements on their wealth, occupation, public office, celebrity, or fame (cf. Goffman 1959). All of the positive and negative ritual practices discussed so far could be re-examined for how externally-based attributes bear upon the sense of propriety. Ritual performances accord to highly nuanced facts of particularity, in this case, to those attributes that people claim for themselves despite the fact that these attributes are external to the current encounter. This means that our felt sense of veneration and honor, of respect, of worth and value, comes partly from such attributes. And, when we decide the appropriate amount of positive or negative ritual, deciding how much distance we must maintain or how much ritual due is in order, we base some of that decision on such attributes.

This issue is one of the thorniest, stickiest wickets of the chapter: it is the problem of being open and honest in our recognition of differential treatment according to externally-based attributes. With great alertness and eyes wide open, we need to look at how people in the modern Western world rely upon externally-based attributes for portioning off of each person's slice of sacredness. Before proceeding any further, I want to say that I am not advocating these practices of regard. In fact, chapter 6 will outline an alternative orientation to externally-based attributes. At present, I am merely trying to describe the normative ritual practices in modern U.S. culture.

Who gets to say the "N-word"? Apparently, the word takes on a different ritual meaning when uttered by members of one race rather than another. And even here, what seems to be appropriate for one person seems highly inappropriate when said by someone. When grandpa uses the "F-word" we tolerate it, even if he comes off as an "old coot" or "a foul-mouthed crank." But if a little girl utters the same word, we may take offense, scold, and punish her. For some reason relating to the sense of ritual order, a man passing gas in public seems different than a woman doing the same (of course depending upon the occasion and the current relation-states among those present). But it is not just age, sex, and race, though these are admittedly drenched in ritual meaning. There are countless other attributes that bear upon the sense of propriety: occupation, status, celebrity.

Part of the challenge that emerged in chapter 1 was that senses of worth and value have become heavily reliant upon externally-based attributes, in particular (wealth, occupation, or status). Chapter 2 took pains to show that these are questionable disambiguations at the very least. And *The Absolute and Universal Occasion*, the grand and mysterious unfolding that lurks behind all mundane social orders, is an eternally recoverable horizon. Walker Percy trenchantly observes that most awkward social encounters, such as executives having to share the bathroom with interns and junior staff, vanish amidst genuine crises and turmoil.[19] By our recognition of this, which functional anonymity and consumer capitalism have largely covered over, we can find a path back to more viable and sustainable sources of significance.

In summary of the three lines of regard, each bears upon the traditions of positive and negative ritual, and taken together, they help to ratify the sacredness of humans and their dealings. The sense of sacredness that appears across all of the examples is mostly felt by the sense of comparative value and worth, finding some people to be deeply cherished, others venerated, while other people are looked-down-upon, perhaps even stigmatized.

Occasion

> Main involvement: reason for the interaction
> Side involvements: latitude from the main involvement
>> Ethos

Current Relation-States

> Relations to: (relative friend, spouse, boss, stranger, enemy, etc.)
> The Other's sense of those same relations

Externally-Based Attributes

> One's own age, sex, race, wealth, occupation, reputation, celebrity
> Other's age, sex, race, wealth, occupation, reputation, celebrity

Figure 4.2. Occasion, Current Relation-States, Externally-Based Attributes

Face-to-face encounters embody a dialogic structure: people ritually laminate their dealings by acting within the canons of self-modesty and self-respect. Goffman eloquently articulates how this ritualization of dealings serves personal and social functions:

> One way of mobilizing the individual for this purpose {to be a self-regulating social participant} is through ritual; {the individual} is taught to be perceptive, to have feelings attached to self and a self expressed through face, to have pride, honor, and dignity, to have considerateness, to have tact, and a certain amount of poise…These rules, when followed, determine the evaluations he will make of himself and of his fellow participants in the encounter, the distribution of his feelings, and the kinds of practices he will employ to maintain a specified and obligatory kind of ritual equilibrium. (Goffman 1967, 44-45)

Again, the underlying logic is an appeal to sacredness, and it is this sacrosanctity that necessitates an array of ceremonial observances. Ritual practices enable people to have the adequate communicative space for character to be accomplished and experienced. Spoken exchanges (or the lack thereof) are not, therefore, simply activities of "information exchange," but rather, they are ritualistic encounters between and among a hierarchy of angels.

Interpersonal Ritual as Heroic-Expiation

I have tried to elucidate a central theme throughout the writings of Erving Goffman: the ritual dimensions of encounters, the displays of respect and regard that overlay and regulate the human face-to-face interaction. Goffman's writings make clear that spoken interaction is no less ritualized than is any other human dealing, and hence it is "something that must be pursued with ritual care" (Goffman 1967, 36). We are not at all similar to machines transmitting information to other machines. We are self-understanding beings, meaning that we are subject to more than factual violence and physical pain; we are open to experiences of violation and even dehumanization.

As face-to-face interaction poses hazards and challenges to a sustained sense of self-worth for all members, most of our spoken moments are laminated with some kind of evidence for the fairness or unfairness of our current situations and other grounds for sympathy, praise, or understanding. And in turn, listeners fulfill their obligation by offering a show of appropriate appreciation and mutual regard. Even conversations of purely instrumental value are overlaid and saturated with ceremonial observances, ritual displays through which reverence for the sacred is instantiated. The many little rituals that couch our "message transmissions" comprise the embodied texture, the symbolic space, through and in which self is negotiated and experienced. Goffman turns our attention to the sacred nature of human interaction when he writes:

> Many gods have been done away with, but the individual himself stubbornly remains as a deity of considerable importance. He walks with some dignity

and is the recipient of many little offerings. He is jealous of the worship due him, yet, approached in the right spirit, he is ready to forgive those who may have offended him. Because of their status relative to his, some persons will find him contaminating while others will find they contaminate him, in either case finding that they must treat him with ritual care. Perhaps the individual is so viable a god because he can actually understand the ceremonial significance of the way he is treated, and quite on his own can respond dramatically to what is proffered him. In contacts between such deities there is no need for middlemen; each of these gods is able to serve as his own priest. (1967, 95)

Regarding the significance of Goffman's scholarship Becker writes, "...the work of Erving Goffman... showed with such consummate art how people impart to one another the daily sense of importance each needs, not with rivalry and boasting, but rather elaborate rules for protecting their insides against social damage and deflation" (1975, 13-14). We find that petty and vain one-upmanship is not the root motive of ritual practices. On the contrary, it is the felt sense of veneration and the sense that persons, as sacred beings, can be desecrated.

We should here recall Figure 1 from chapter 1. The schema characterizes two broad meaning horizons emergent from ritual and monetary practices within modern U.S. culture. Ritual, we can recall, refers to all the ways that value and worth are conveyed in both natural and social engagements. Money, on the other hand, has value and worth as defined by economic exchange rates. But the separation is not so simple, as many ritual practices today require money, and money earning and spending are also caught up in ritual dimensions.[20] They have grown together, and each is operative within the other; they can be extricated from each other only in theoretical analysis. This means that the possibility of cosmic relevance remains mostly covered over, largely degenerated into the contemporary culture of self-pandering.

At the very least, modern Western culture has witnessed the rise of D.I.N.Ks (dual income no kids). This means that increasing numbers of people are choosing to not have children, and many of these people do so despite being self-consciously aware of not being able to escape their own death. So, the question becomes: Without belief in an afterlife, and without even the promise of continuance through progeny, what are the horizons of significance other than the low-visioned self-serving wealth accumulation and/or other than enlisting in the war machine or other fundamentalisms? Granted, unless or until technological progress completely removes all possibilities of cultivating care (i.e., unless it dissolves all "forms of recalcitrance," extracts all "coefficients of adversity," and eradicates all practices of gift-giving and sacrifice), ritualistic guilt expiation will continue to occur somewhat "naturally." But can't we at least recognize and outline the prospects of some horizons of meaning that are richer than materialist accumulationism?

What would it mean if people were to value reading, serious study, and the cultivation of one's mind? How about diligence in handicrafts and artistic works, or people whose legs ache from yesterday's dance practice? How about a world where people, having gained the courage to need little, explicitly recognize their need to give and spend all of their lives in a self-disciplined quest for a small but well cultivated garden, the fruits of which they generously share? Here we begin to imagine the horizons of the neo-Stoic cosmopolitan, someone practicing the arts of extra-mundane heroism, the arts of worldly rejuvenation.

Notes

1   And it should never be forgotten that propriety is always, at least to some degree, ambiguous and takes its form through some kind of authoritative disambiguation.

2   We find this to provide a substantial challenge to those who would reduce Goffman's ideas to the study of situational improprieties. There may well be a good deal of humor had in bringing about situational improprieties. These may even have some value in challenging the status quo. Nonetheless, we must understand that abjectly desecrating oneself (the ultimate in impropriety) is the exemplar of mental illness. And so, even if persons have a special license to handle criticisms of themselves made by their own hands, they are not free to make public improprieties of which they are the butt of the joke without encumbering some stigma.

3   Goffman, (1963a, 161).

4   Goffman, (1963b, 45).

5   Goffman, (1959, 177-187).

6   Goffman, (1974, 215).

7   Goffman, (1963a, 33-35).

8   Goffman, (1971, 122-125).

9   Goffman, (1971, 83).

10   cf. Goffman, (1974, 210), esp. note 15 on Bateson's notion of metacommunication.

11   A commonly replayed comic bit can be found regarding the awkward embarrassment of false-start farewells: heartfelt good-byes are given only to have the person need to return momentarily for something.

12   Goffman, (1971, 95-187).

13   cf. Goffman, (1963a, 103) and (1967, 120).

14   Consider the fact that there are ritual demands against talking to oneself in public, and moreover that "to be seen walking down the street alone while *silently* gesticulating a conversation with an absent other is as much a breach as talking aloud to ourselves" (Goffman 1981, 87).

15   A central difficulty in any attempt to discuss the ritual order is that what is "appropriate" varies not only according to who said what, but to who said what while who else was listening, or even, when who did not say what to whom.

16   For an interesting discussion of some of the difficulties in doing so, see "Alienation from Interaction," in *Interaction Ritual* (1967, 113-136).

17 Arguably the television show "Seinfeld" is a gold mine of simple, mundane, ritual improprieties. Next time you find yourself laughing as you watch "Seinfeld" ask yourself, "What breach of ceremonial order is occurring?"

18 cf. Goffman, (1961b, 31-33).

19 Cf. Percy's (1954) wonderful account of the "Loss of Sovereignty" in his chapter "The Loss of the Creature" and also see his account of "shyness" and social anxiety in his *Lost in the Cosmos* (1983).

20 Cf. Hugh Dalziel Duncan's (1962) discussions of "The Social Rhetoric of Money: Simmel and Veblen" and "Spending as Prayer: the American Christmas."

"This, after all is said and done, is the only real problem of life, the only worthwhile preoccupation of man: what is one's true talent, his secret gift, his authentic vocation? In what way is one truly unique, and how can he express this uniqueness, give it form, dedicate it to something beyond himself?" (Becker 1973, 82)

> *"Man's most characteristic attribute,*
> *his conscious orientation toward the future,*
> *implies a willingness to make the effort required*
> *for shaping his personality and thereby his destiny."*
> *(René Dubos, 48).*

CHAPTER 5

BARTERING AS RITUAL OF TRANSCENDENCE

As tribal rituals for regenerating the cosmos have all but dwindled away, a main fear today is not having enough money. By the lights of many people, few things could be worse. And, as a correlate, money has become the predominant or even sole pursuit for many individuals. It serves as the basic motive behind everyday dealings: if not for the income provided, people would engage in something else. The popular expression "making something of oneself" has therefore come to mean, almost exclusively, helping oneself to become financially secure and self-sufficient. But even those who have accumulated great amounts of capital and possessions and who live a life of luxury and ease have not by this ensured meaningfulness in their lives. In fact, well-to-do people can remain troubled and unfulfilled, leading, as Thoreau said, "lives of quiet desperation."

Consider too that by the standard of material comforts, many U.S. citizens live as ancient peoples imagined the gods to live. They enjoy comforts, countless conveniences, and generally, a life of ease. With all of this, many people remain unfulfilled, unhappy, or even miserable.[1] Why? Could it partly be because so much is provided for them? So much "technological progress" has meant less adversity, more comfort, and greater ease, and it continually promises that people will get more and more for less and less effort. The question is: Is this really in people's best interest? Or, more pointedly asked: who, exactly, considers this to be progress?

The present study, I have been trying to show, is highly instructive on this issue: People need self-esteem and they need to expiate the guilt of being human. They need to sense that they have not squandered nor trivialized the very gift of their lives. They need to believe that they have something to give as well as feel that they have, in fact, adequately given. They need both heroism *and* expiation, which implies that people's lives gain significance not by being provided for nor by securing material comforts, but rather, when individuals are called to sacrifice self and talents for something beautiful, grand, or noble.

Saint-Ex and his Citadelle

Earlier, summarizing changes from primitive economics to modern money economies, I underscored Ernest Becker's claim that, "we can no longer be redeemed by work, since the creation of a surplus is no longer addressed as a gift to the gods" (1975, 89). I now re-evaluate this claim by turning to the writings of Antoine de Saint-Exupéry (Saint-Ex). I try to unveil "redeeming" dimensions of work by carefully considering the "unusable surplus of beauty" within any job well done. To the extent that people yearn for cosmic significance and eternality, Saint-Ex helps to sketch an ideal hero: someone who crafts in the image of perfection, and, for recompense, "becomes eternal, no longer dreading death." Meaningful labor, I will try to show, remains a vital horizon for cultivating a neo-Stoic heroism. The present chapter accordingly examines how "bartering" (i.e., labor activities and work involvements transformed into ritual mortification) offers vital horizons for the generation of human significance.

Before advancing on, I want to give some background on Saint-Exupéry and discuss how he might have used his own writing as a horizon of bartering. Saint-Ex was born at the turn of the century to a noble family near Lyons, France. He spent his childhood in luxury, dwelling in the magnificent Chateau de La Mole and the Chateau of Saint-Maurice (Cate 1970). His comfortable adolescence turned to wistful depression as he reached young adulthood, for although he was old enough to live on his own, he was quite unhappy and had great difficulty in selecting a career. He wrote many letters to his mother, and his only income for some time was the money he received in her responses. Despite having his material needs met, he knew his life lacked genuine meaning and significance (Cate 1970). Without a call to a greater mission, he felt ennui cast upon him, which he later recounts as his "comfortable conditions were but a lack" (de Saint-Exupéry 1950, 110).

Saint-Ex found many truths about the human condition to be paradoxical. For example, people's lives became most meaningful when they accepted submission to something greater than themselves. This paradoxical insight came to a head for him when World War I broke out and he joined France's forces. He there felt alive as he often risked his life in unstable and untested airplanes (Migeo 1960). But alas, when the war ended and Saint-Ex again was living as a civilian, he languished from the sense of not serving something greater than himself. Here I should point out that he received wide acclaim for his novels and yet this was not enough to keep him from enlisting in the French forces when World War II broke out. During WWII, helping to establish and maintain postal lines along the Western coast of Africa, he spent a great deal of time alone in the heavens looking down upon the earth. He also had many adventures where he actually risked his life to help others in distress. In his posthumously published reflections, *A Sense of Life*, Saint-Ex wrote,

> We are children of the age of comfort, yet we are filled with an inexpressible happiness when we share our last crust with others in the desert. To those of us who have known the joy of rescuing a crew downed in the Sahara, all other pleasures seem empty. (1965, 154)

Thus, the times in his life that were most meaningful were those when he sacrificed and risked for something vaster than himself, while the times when he was most disconsolate were those when he lived as a sedentary serving none but himself, a person whose only task was to amass a store of worldly goods and comforts.

About his final work, *Citadelle* (trans., *The Wisdom of the Sands*, or *WS*),[2] Saint-Ex referred to it as his *magnum opus* and he declared that all other works were but practice for this one (cf. Cate 1970). It was the object for which he made himself a barter, the grand poem that he continued perfecting. At the very heart of this beautiful work lies a deeply felt concern over the quality of life: it eloquently ruminates upon what each person might know or become to increase the significance of being alive. As both author and mail carrier, Saint-Ex knew the impact of the written word. In a letter to a friend, he writes,

> "I do not mind being killed in war,"… "What will remain of all I loved? I am thinking as much of customs, certain intonations that can never be replaced, a certain spiritual light. Of luncheons at a Provençal farm under the olive-trees; but of Handel, too. As for the material things, I don't care a damn if they survive or not. What I value is a certain arrangement of these things. Civilization is an invisible boon; it concerns not the things we see but the unseen bonds linking these together in one special way and not otherwise…Anyhow, if I come out of it alive, there will be only one problem I shall set myself: What can one, what *must* one, say to men?" (de Saint-Exupéry 1950, vii).

We remain unable to determine what Saint-Ex himself ultimately would have done with the book; some authorities suggest that it might have been published in a different form, or not published at all.[3] To this we must add that it was least similar to his earlier works and was hardly a widely appreciated work.[4] A masterpiece of articulacy and beauty, *WS* obliquely demonstrates how Saint-Ex learned to take the art of writing itself (not the fame nor money that it earned him) as the horizon of self-sacrifice, as a practice of ritual mortification.

As prelude to the larger analysis of this chapter—and in an effort to illustrate how labor (and admittedly, even activities involving money) might be more potently magnified in their ritual dimensions—let me round off this introduction with one extended quotation from *WS*.

To contextualize this quotation, I should say that the story within *WS* tells of a chieftain's son who, after the recent assassination of his father, must take leadership of the citadel. Out in the desert, the new chieftain must learn to govern his people and find the words to help them. He interprets the assassination not as one leading to the downfall of the empire, but rather as a symptom of his people losing sight of the "knot-eternal," that which makes sheep, mountains, and people a single, unified domain. With much critical reflection and deeply felt responsibility for the quality of people's lives, the young chieftain assumes his mission: learning what he must say to his people.

The chieftain does not offer a direct and unwavering answer to the many issues related to leading his people into meaningful lives. Rather, he poses issues in many different forms and answers them in many different ways. In this particular excerpt the chieftain decides to walk among his people and, by careful observation, identify those who are happy from those who are not as well as discern the reasons therein. Here is only a tiny fragment of his observations and conclusions:

> This I have learned, which is essential: that it behooves us to begin by building the ship and equipping the caravan, and erecting the temple which outlasts men. For, once this is done, you shall see them gladly bartering themselves for that which is more precious than themselves. Painters, gravers, silversmiths, will arise. But place no hope in man if he works for his own lifetime and not his eternity…

> Thus it was that, walking amongst my people in the loom of the nightfall, when all things fall asunder, seeming them seated on the thresholds of their humble booths, in their work-worn garments, and resting from their bee-like toil, I took less thought for them than for the honeycomb on which daylong they had worked conjointly. And, pausing before one who was blind and furthermore had lost a limb, I pondered. So old, so near the grave was he, groaning like a rusty mill-wheel when he moved…yet ever he was becoming more and more luminous, brighter, apter for the task for which he had made the barter of himself. With trembling hands he continued perfecting his fretwork, which had become for him as an elixir, ever subtler and more potent. Thus, escaping by a miracle from his gnarled old flesh, he was growing ever happier, more and more invulnerable. More and more imperishable. And, dying, knew it not, his hands being full of stars.

> Thus toiled they all their lives, building up a treasure not for daily use and bartering themselves for things of beauty incorruptible; allotting only a small

part of their toil to daily needs, and all the rest to their carvings, to the unusable virtue of chased gold or silver, the perfection of form, the grace of noble curves—all of which served no purpose save to absorb that part of themselves they bartered, and which outlasts mortality....

In my long night walks it was revealed to me that the quality of my empire's civilization rests not upon its material benefits but on men's obligations and the zeal they bring to their tasks. It derives not from owning but from giving. Civilized is that craftsman I have spoken of, who remakes himself in the thing he works on, and, for his recompense, becomes eternal, no longer dreading death...But those who content themselves with luxury bought from the merchants are none the better for it—even though they feast there eyes only on perfection—if, to begin with, they themselves have created nothing. Well I know those tribes degenerate who no longer write their poems but only read them; who no longer till their fields, but have recourse to slaves... No love have I for the sluggards, the sedentaries of the heart; for those who barter nothing *become* nothing. Life will not have served to ripen them. For them Time flows like a handful of sand and wears them down. What will I have to make over to God on their account?...For grief is ever begotten of Time that, flowing, has not shaped its fruit....

Going a little farther...I saw, too, my one-legged cobbler busy threading gold into his leathren slippers and, weak as was his voice, I guessed that he was singing.

"What is it, cobbler, that makes you so happy?"

But I heeded not the answer; for I knew that he would answer me amiss and prattle of money he had earned, or his meal, or the bed awaiting him— knowing not that his happiness came of his transfiguring himself into golden slippers. (1950, 29-33)

I now outline a few of the many insights nestled within this finely crafted passage; I offer a bit of the wisdom regarding bartering and human significance available therein.

First, the *quality* of civilization rests not in material benefits, but on people's obligations and the zeal they bring to their tasks. Prosperity is not measured by owning or buying, but by the extent to which people barter themselves for things of beauty incorruptible. We should scorn and forewarn the sluggards and sedentaries of the heart; those who fail to barter fail to *become*. Such persons are led into grief and come to live out their days dreading death. People are not only a fruit that may or may not ripen, their ripening depends upon their strivings toward perfection in heart, mind, and deed. Civilizations are basically soul groves for growing ambrosia; our basic duty is to struggle to become worthy of harvest and consumption by the gods. This means that spiritual radiance grows slowly, takes times to cultivate. It is the gift bestowed upon those who have committed to crafts that can take entire lifetimes to perfect. The peculiar kind of steeping necessary for ripening souls involves the practice and habit of gathering time while moving toward an image of perfection.

Second, people can best aspire to greatness and submit to creations that transcend them in time and beauty, only when they feel called upon to serve a larger visage. They need to have something grander than themselves to which they can submit. By fastening on to what transcends them, their individuating labor and efforts are meaningfully enfolded. The metaphors of "ship," "caravan," and "temple" point to the totalities that surpass and enwrap individuals, the larger wholes to which human creations stand as an homage and in which they are secured. In erecting a temple that outlasts any person, we establish something worthy of sacrifice and without which people languish in self-service. They can stagnate into lives that serve but one lifetime. The one-legged cobbler, by focusing all attention upon the fine gold lacing within his work, transcended his own existence.

Third, by creating objects of more than practical use (and for more than for their own lifetimes), people transcend their deaths. This is what I mean by the notion of "bartering." To barter is to sacrifice oneself for one's craft or vital program. And, when our paintings, dances, carvings, and handicrafts are placed above our daily needs, the objects themselves absorb us; we barter our bodies and our time into the unusable virtue of chased gold or silver, the perfection of form, and grace of noble curves. Sacrifice, perfection, and eternity, these are vital components of bartering. In suffering and sacrificing to create objects of beauty incorruptible, people move toward the eternal. But the point is not to have things created and standing as monuments to individuals. The point is not that each of us should work hard *so as to be remembered*, though being remembered also may happen. People outlast their own mortality by using the object of the barter as a receptacle and a vehicle, a bridge through which they crossover. It is by becoming civilized, meaning people who remake themselves in the things they work on, and, for their recompense, become eternal, no longer dreading death. As a further cautionary note, I want to underscore this is not a prescription or sanction to reduce civilization to producing only perfection. It is intended to urge the love and zeal for creating beautiful things. Love of the well-danced dance is not to be used as a reason for condemning or forbidding the badly danced dance; bad sculptures are accepted on the grounds that they are the forcing bed upon which great sculptures emerge. To rule out all but the perfect begets not a civilization but a museum, for only the dead are perfect.

Fourth, most persons fail to fully realize from where their happiness comes. At two different points, the same metaphor is cast: we not only find someone dying, [who] knew it not, his hand being full of stars, we also find a one-legged cobbler who, though answering amiss regarding the source of his happiness, was transfiguring himself into golden slippers. In both of these cases, bartering is the vehicle of transcendence, even though it can pass below conscious awareness.

More generally cast, then, technological progress and material comforts do not directly equal a meaningful life. Pleasure and ease are not happiness and significance. Said even more strongly, pleasure may in fact be important, but it is not what people are seeking when they seek a significant life. The visage of beauty wrought from solid marble, or clay shaped in a hymn of perfection, or dances that moves audiences to tears, these are the ritual overflows of bartering. Unfortunately, more than a few people in today's society depict their dream job as one that is easy, fun, has little responsibility, and that, of course, pays very well. They speak of wanting more pay for less work. Some even comically suggest that it would be nice to get paid handsomely for doing nothing. And, perhaps not surprisingly, these same people are likely to be bored on weekends. They fail to see in work as well as in free time the possibility of worldly rejuvenation; they seem not to recognize how bartering is that horizon within our labors that transforms any work into an act of expiative-heroism.

Citadellean Themes

The preceding can be summarized and the remains previewed by suggesting that humans dwell in realms that are "invisible to the eye." It is for this reason that the human world is always extra-mundane. It does not just consist of material things, but also of invisible meanings, significances that rule each person's heart. Looking down at a child in a playground with a broken toy at her feet and tears running down her cheeks, we too might suddenly be moved to tears, not because of the child's tears, but because the child's tears open to a world that is unseen. More than a little girl crying over a broken toy, she is *participating in the sorrows of humanity*. It is thus essential to see all material things as opening to something vaster than themselves. As the chieftain states, "A solitary flower can be a window opening on the vision of spring" (de Saint-Exupéry 1950, 85). Two additional illustrations from *The Little Prince*, Saint-Ex's most famous book, may help to clarify this point as well as pave the way for my continued analysis.

Saint-Ex writes that when he was a young boy he had read a story about boa constrictors that said that boas swallowed their prey whole, without chewing. The young Saint-Ex thought about this, drew a picture of a boa digesting an elephant, and then showed his "masterpiece to the grown-ups, and asked them whether the drawing frightened them. But they answered: 'Frighten? Why should any one be frightened by a hat?'"(de Saint-Exupéry 1943, 7-8). The grown-ups, he recounts, were unable to see past the surface of the drawing; all they saw was a picture of a hat. Saint-Ex further writes that he saved that drawing and showed it now and again to people he had met, as a sort of test for friendship.[5]

The theme of invisibility is touched upon again as Saint-Ex is dying of dehydration after several days in the desert. He tells of his discussion with the little prince regarding the meaning of the desert:

> "What makes the desert beautiful," said the little prince, "is that somewhere it hides a well." I was astonished by a sudden understanding of the mysterious radiation of the sands. When I was a little boy I lived in an old house, and legend told that a treasure was buried there. To be sure, no one had ever known how to find it; perhaps no one had ever even looked for it. But it cast an enchantment over that house. My home was hiding a secret in the depths of its heart... "Yes" I said to the little prince. "The house, the stars, the desert—what gives them their beauty is something that is invisible!" (de Saint-Exupéry 1943, 75-76)

If we are to understand the nature of human significance, we must be willing to look beyond our eyes. We must learn to register what remains hidden, for human significance dwells in the pervasively unseen.

Presented here, distilled from *WS*, is a rough model of ritual mortification as worldly rejuvenation. The model attunes to those horizons of bartering that, taken together, align with others, space, and time. To labor or dance or craft something with an image of perfection, trying to imagine its contributions to others in the history of the world while also imagining its continued presence in the future, this is bartering at its fullest attenuation (also cf. Thayer 1988).

Bartering: Surplus Beauty as Gift to the Gods

To barter, as meant here, is to trade oneself for objects of "beauty incorruptible." By diligently laboring for some mission that transcends petty practical concerns, by sacrificing self as we strive for some ideal, true love, or some image of perfection, we enjoy the outpouring of significance that flows from the bartering. It is a supreme act of heroism-expiation.

Much of the chieftain's ruminations involve describing the beauty of people spending their lives perfecting their arts. This he came to see as the essence of the human condition. In caring for a certain object and in meeting natural adversity and resistance, we neglect other objects as we must invest ourselves into one relation and not another. People often give of themselves, committing themselves to be virtuosos in their handiwork, and devote long hours to perfecting some pottery, a cloth, or a poem. A more subtle implication is that many things of the world can seem to be separated or at a distance (e.g., water and absence of water, good and evil, friend and foe, beloved and absence), but they remain invisibly connected and those invisible connections can be used to generate significance. Denying that we must select between terms that "stick out their tongues at each other," we can agree with the chieftain where he states, "I am weary of words that flout each other in vain contention; nor does it seem to me preposterous if I find in the quality of my constraints the quality of my freedom" (1950, 239). We need be careful, therefore, not to grab hold of only one side of polar elements, for in doing so we extinguish the significance of both sides. Said more positively, significance can be amplified by pulling opposites away from each other and thereby adding to the potency of each.

A life where all is provided but nothing is asked in return may be a life of easily obtained ends, but this is not a significant life. It is a life no better than that of domesticated cattle. People need more than having their needs met; we need more than being provided for. Expressed numerous times, in many different ways throughout *WS* is the idea that, "What nourishes human hearts is not what they get from the wheat, but what they give to the wheat." This further means that

> It is in boring wells, in achieving a day of rest, in winning the diamond from the earth and in love that your true riches lie. But not in owning wells, in having days of rest, or diamonds, or love at will. Even as you are none the better for merely desiring these things, without striving towards them. (1950, 231)

We gain only where we give, and our continued obligation cannot be outstripped. This point is beautifully brought out where the chieftain recalls his early instruction regarding the importance of bartering. His father led him out to watch three thousand refugees camp outside the citadel. Being kind yet not having room for all of them, his father "Furnished them with food and clothing, tea and sugar; but asked no work of them in return for his munificence" (1950, 51). The refugees, able only to receive, became listless, and, by having nothing to overcome, nothing against which to shape themselves, they became apathetic, sickly, and decadent. These people turned into "mere husks," lost the significance of their lives by no longer giving of themselves, and from that experience the following lesson was distilled: "If you wish them to be brothers, have them build a tower. But if you would have them hate each other, throw them corn" (1950, 52).

We too often trust our senses rather than our hearts. We may really believe that we want to be, as it were, sedentary. We may believe that what we want is less responsibility, greater comforts, and more material goods. Amassed material goods are very visible to the eye, yet the significance of such objects often relates to the amount of effort it took to "win" them. Taking care of a particular object, one imbues that object with significance. The fox, in *The Little Prince*, sums up this idea when he states, "It is only with the heart that one can see rightly; what is essential is invisible to the eye" (de Saint-Exupéry 1943, 70). The fox explains to the little prince that by spending time with a thing, it becomes special and unique. Because of our previous bartering for them, many things of the world have sacramental vestiges. One of the characters in the *WS*, reporting about an arduous journey across the sea, says to the chieftain:

> But, Sire, I make bold to say, not one of us feared death; we all feared for our foolish little things. We were discovering that life has a meaning only if one barters it day by day for something other than itself. Thus the death of the gardener does no harm to the tree; but if you threaten the tree the gardener dies twice. (1950, 26)

This lesson of bartering, although it seems so obvious in this context, quickly and easily recedes from view, for people can grow blind to the sources of significance within their lives. They can even do what is counter to them. They can believe that their happiness comes from diamonds that have not been wrought by tearing fingers on stone. This also means that

> …wherever the good things of the world are most abundant men have more chance of deceiving themselves as to the nature of their joys…Whereas, being without possessions, those of the desert and the monastery can make no mistake as to whence their joys derive; and thus it is easier for them to keep unscathed the source of their fervor. (1950, 235-236)

Don't misunderstand me. People of the desert and monastery are not necessarily any happier than other people, but, in having no material wealth, they are much less likely to be fooled about the sources of their happiness. Bored listlessness awaits "… tribes degenerate who no longer write their poems but only read them; who no longer till their fields, but have recourse to slaves" (1950, 30). The more that any civilization becomes filled with people who listen to music yet play no instrument, who watch dance but do not dance themselves, who enjoy looking at pieces of art and handiwork but have created none with their own hands, the more that that civilization is dying. Its people will come to languish in the dull and easy comforts of insignificant, stall-fed, life.

Temples, Caravans, Domains, and Tabernacles

Bartering is done for something greater than ourselves, something to which we can become a fragment, something to which we can sacrifice ourselves.[6] Depending on the larger wholes served, the same gestures and actions take quite differ-ent levels of fervor and significance, and hence, the mostly invisible difference between manual labor and acts of bartering.

> I send out my prisoners to break stones. And the stones they break are void of meaning. But if you are building your house, is it not quite otherwise with the stones you break? You are setting up a wall, and your gestures bespeak not a punishment but a hymn. (1950, 185)

It is not simply the visible actions—but what those actions are believed to be serving—that give objects, lives, and domains their particular significance. Ob-jects also take on significance as they become enshrined within vaster domains. The entire tree is in every flower of the tree, and the great cedar gives its limbs their particular significance. Human significance flows to people who see those larger wholes in which they are immersed; they feel the significance flowing from their membership within them.

Of no small importance is architecture. Architects and planners need to care-fully consider their role in elevating the human spirit. Those who create human dwellings play a pivotal role in any culture's sense of identity and place within the cosmos. Homes are more than just a place to stay, and in fact, people need much more than simply private and safe spaces. "For I have lit on a great truth: to wit, that all men *dwell*, and life's meaning changes for them with the meaning of the home" (1950, 15).[7] If people are to richly experience the full dimensions of human significance, they need to view the heavens and to see the stars; they need dwellings so magnificent, so transcendent, that they resonate with the awesome-ness of existing. The chieftain accordingly spoke to his architects:

> True, it is urgent that man should eat, for else he cannot live, and death abides no question. Yet love, the sense of life and the quest of God are more impor-tant. No thoughts waste I on a breed that merely fills its belly…Thus I blame not the priority you give to things of daily need; but I blame you for making them your end…he {a denizen} needs the great Milky Way above him and the vast sea spaces, though neither stars nor ocean serve his daily needs. (1950, 76-77)

People need to recognize their place in the cosmos, and, with that, develop a deeper sense of humanity, a sense of their spiritual essence. Nonetheless, people still can betray their humanity by the words they speak, and then, given the many comforts of modern life, they easily lose sight of what is essential for a thriving civilization: zeal for a task in which one bartered one's very existence for perfec-tion.

The chieftain tells of the cross-eyed prophet, who, thinking it best to eradicate those parts of the domain he sees as evil, asks the chieftain to rid the kingdom of them. The chieftain laughs, seeing this person's inability to recognize that his wish, if granted, would destroy the essence of his life. The chieftain thought of this man, "It is on evil that he thrives. Without it where would he be?" (1950, 217). Unable to see the unity within diversity, his people set out to remove what they saw as injustices. Eliminating those whom each sees fit, people often undo themselves by expunging what they believed to be antithetical. They seem not to grasp how opposition gives purpose and constructs form.

A related dialectical paradox is that when we are free to serve only ourselves, our lives lack significance; footsteps lack the weight of the world when only personal concerns occupy mind and deed. Inversely, a life submitted to some greater enterprise floods relevance and enrichment. So, then, a residual challenge is that, "If each man chooses the site of the temple for himself, and places his stone wherever he thinks fit, you will never see a temple, only a huddle of stones. For creation requires oneness" (1950, 192). As unpopular as the notion has become in recent decades, hierarchical forms are natural structures that facilitate significance and transcendence: the whole makes the individual parts meaningful, not vice versa. For these reasons we can better understand why the chieftain suggests,

> Thus it is with the empire. I have not made a god of the empire so that it should reduce men to servitude... I stablish the empire so as to fulfill men and inspire them with it, and for me the empire counts less than the man. It is in order to stablish men that I subordinate them to the empire; I do not subordinate men so as to stablish the empire. (1950, 138)

People's lives become more significant as they think of themselves as members of a domain. If people are unable to discern the image of the larger whole from the many diverse elements, they drag out their lives in petty cares and concerns. The chieftain thus proclaims, "I would have you form part of a tree, and subordinated to the tree. I would have your pride lodged in the tree, and likewise your life, so that it may possess a meaning" (1950, 286).[8]

Enabling a vision of the whole for all people, even those whose lives appear to contradict, is no small task. Indeed, how to create a vision that allows people to become as one, the oneness that is a bartering of one's all to some ideal of perfection? Central to enabling this vision is to maintain differences yet establish equal value. People must come to recognize that merely looking alike does not mean equality. What is essential is that individuals bring the full passion of giving to their tasks, not that each is responsible for the same task, "To unify is to bind in an ever firmer knot the diversities of sundry things, not to efface them for the sake of a symmetry leading nowhere" (1950, 181). We find both diversity as well as equality, therefore, when each person equally barters for the image of beauty incorruptible. "Even as the stone is submissive not to the other stones but to the temple. When you serve, it is creation you are serving" (1950, 271). Thus, one possible way to enable unity within and throughout apparent diversity is to let the unusable beauty created along the way to be the keystone of the temple.

Traditions and Habits as Weight of the Past

Cultures themselves depend upon people being able to appreciate the significance of their obligations, and this is made possible as current generations instill in youth an appreciation for their heritages.[9] By knowing their origins, people feel an inertia or weight of the previous generation, and this heaviness can be harnessed as a source of significance. Reflecting upon his people and their relations to the past, the chieftain thought,

> And I saw how incumbent was the tradition of my empire, requiring every man to hand down or to take over his inheritance, as the case may be. For I want dwellers in my land, not campers who come from anywhere and nowhere. (1950, 250)

If people are to appreciate their placement within larger wholes, they must see how their bartering contributes to that whole, and they need to be opened to the full historical breadth and cosmic scope of their participations. The actual civilizing of any civilization depends upon successfully transmitting the unseen vision of unity that emanates from the diversity of visible things. If any culture changes too rapidly and too quickly abandons the past, successive generations within the culture will become blind to the knot emanating from previous generations. Children, if not properly inculcated, will come to feel as wayfarers and will be denied entire horizons of meaning and significance. Hence:

> You shall build your children in your image, lest in later days they come to drag their lives out joylessly in a land which will seem to them but an empty camping place, and whose treasure they will allow to rot away uncared-for, because they have not been given its keys. (1950, 251)

For those who are concerned with the experience of human significance, a key issue is tradition and its potential erosion in contemporary consumer capitalism.[10]

But the weight of the past poses its own difficulties, for people also can struggle to change acquired bad habits and long-standing social injustices. It is hard to deny that, often times, our acts do not bring significance or happiness, but we persist only because we are accustomed to acting that way. Once people get to be a certain way, they wish to continue in that way.

> You crave for that alone which is a condition of your permanence. The man
> whom strong drink has stablished craves for strong drink. (Not that he is the
> better for it; indeed he dies of it.) One who has been molded by your civiliza-
> tion craves for your civilization. The supreme instinct is that of permanence;
> it rules even the life instinct. (1950, 291)

The theme of permanence runs throughout *WS* and is summed up in the chieftain's proclamation, "For true was my saying that ever a man seeks after what is
weightiest in him" (1950, 168). People's lives come to take on an inertia such
that once things get moving in a certain direction, they seek to continue in that
direction. Knowing that people choose to continue rather than to be happy, the
chieftain tells that he, "Discovered that beggars cling to their stench as to something rare and precious" (1950, 3). This is also why the beggars, "no sooner were
they healed than they found themselves of no account, like barren soil that feeds
nothing; and they made haste to revive the ulcers that formerly had batten on
their flesh" (3). The chieftain likewise reflects upon his father's lessons regarding
the prostitutes of the empire. His father had taken the prostitutes away from their
lives and offered them a different, a more acceptable career. His father spoke,

> "Now I will show you," he said, "what chiefly rules our hearts." He had them
> clad in new garments, and each woman was given a clean, cool house with a
> fountain playing in the courtyard, and, by way of work, fine laces to embroi-
> der. Moreover they were paid so lavishly that they now earned twice what
> they had earned before. Nor would he permit the keeping of any watch on
> them. "So now," he said to me, "we see them happy, this sorry jetsam of the
> deep. Clean, contented, freed from fear." Nevertheless, one after the other,
> they slunk back to the stews. "For," my father said, "they missed their infelic-
> ity. Not by reason of a foolish preference for infelicity instead of happiness,
> but because each of us is drawn ineluctably towards that which is heaviest in
> himself. (1950, 166-167)

Even after new lives have been offered, people tend toward what has become
"weightiest" in them.

Few tasks are as difficult as disposing of an old self and slowly building up
a new one, and we should always be suspicious of people who sell the idea of
quick and easy change. All real change is slow, arduous, and tectonic. Moreover,
people easily fool themselves into thinking that they could be a certain way without establishing that as a way of being. As the chieftain says, "What you do, you
stablish; and that is all. If when progressing towards a certain goal, you make-
believe to move towards another, only he who is the tool of words will think you
clever" (1950, 70). A relevant implication is that people should never practice
what they do not want to become good at. Strategists learn to make bartering a

habit. They learn to keep their temples "pure and bright," even when there is, at present, no divine visitation.

We need to be careful not to assume that the meaning of bartering is to achieve and have secured objects of beauty incorruptible. It is true that people need to feel as if their work will be enshrined and protected for all time, for such a reach toward the future penetrates and amplifies the bartered-for object, but we need to understand that it is the *ongoing act of bartering*, not the objects of the barter, that renders a life significant. An ambiguous tension to be registered, therefore, is that people need a sense of secured permanence and a sense of contribution to the future, and yet to be able, simultaneously, to stand in the ever-fleeting impermanence where there is nothing but the vitality of creation. Although we need to build and dwell in temples that outlast individuals, and we also need to habitually strive for objects of beauty incorruptible, we must also be ready to liquidate the amassed store. For, "the well danced-dance admits no hoarding," and it is the fervor of creating that makes a civilization.

Pearls, Visions, and Thirst for the Future

> For man is so built that, essentially, love is a thirst for love, culture a thirst for culture and the joy of the ceremonial quest of the black pearl, a thirst for the black pearl lying at the bottom of the sea. (1950, 340)

The chieftain tells of a black pearl lying at the bottom of the sea but which no person has yet recovered. Those who spend their days searching for the black pearl are filled with the zeal of the search, for the thought of finding it beckons them to barter their lives to seek it out. Imagination feeds the spirit, and believing in and striving for your heart's ideal, even if you never find it, enriches your life. While his people may need to believe that the black pearl exists, it needs to exist only as their desideratum to yield significance to bartering. As the chieftain writes, "Only the direction has a meaning. It is the going-towards that matters, not the destination; for all journeys end in death" (1950, 150). Grand goals help to anchor and give substance to one's struggles and this further implies:

> But I have seen a constant loser go on playing chess for years, in the fond hope that one day he may have the thrill of victory. Thus, though she on whom your heart is set is not for you, you are the richer for the fact that she exists. (1950, 323)

It is tragic when people no longer strive for things that are unattainable; logic too quickly dupes them into believing that obtaining a particular end is more important than the striving toward that end.

We can note interesting parallels between Becker's "The Spectrum of Lone-liness" and the views of the chieftain. Becker suggests that we are the only crea-ture who feels that it might have been abandoned and that modernity is the luxury of yearning for an absent god.[11] The chieftain offers these remarks about prayer. He concludes that the potency of prayer lies in the absence of a response. He states, "Prayer is fruitful so long as God does not answer" (1950, 145). Through-out the story the chieftain pleads to God for a "fragment of thy cloak" with which to protect his people from their self-destruction. At one point the chieftain, sitting on a mountain top and praying for some advice on how to lead his people, begs God for some sign that He is listening. Knowing how petty his concerns must seem to God, he begs for only the slightest sign. Seeing a crow perched upon a rock near his resting place, the chieftain softly thought, "When I end my prayer, bid that crow take wing, and this will be as it were a nod from another man than myself and I shall no longer feel alone in the world" (1950, 171). Watching the crow out of the corner of his eye as to indicate patience for God, he grew inter-nally anxious as it failed to move. The chieftain then unsuspectingly received a revelation: "And for the first time I perceived that the whole greatness of prayer lies in the fact that no answer is vouchsafed it" (1950, 171). The act of praying is that act of wishing for something unseen, calling for help where none is to be granted. The chieftain urges not for his people to stop praying, but rather recog-nizes the riches of prayer lie in the *act* of praying, not in having prayers answered. Knowing their taking to logic, the chieftain was fearful that his people would not understand.

We might even imagine someone who thinks it fit to remove all unattainable goals. Far from seeing this cure as beneficial to civilization, people should see that such a removal is ultimately in the business of dehumanizing civilization. People who begin with the belief that they will be happier by attempting to re-move all unattainable goals often discover that they unwittingly are extinguishing the very fervor of their lives. Wishing his people to strive to the loftiest of ambi-tions, the chieftain admonishes, "Thus you would allow nothing to exist that is outside your reach. The child stretches his arms towards a star, and cries because he cannot have it. Therefore your justice bids you extinguish the star" (1950, 324). This kind of justice leads to the erosion of the culture itself, as one's place of arrival is secondary to one's actual striving toward a grandiose goal. In fact, "Once completed, your city will die. For these men live not by what they receive but by what they give...And never have I 'completed' my city" (1950, 69). The ultimate attainment of the goal matters not, and may even be a hindrance, for the significance of any goal comes from its ability to conjure dreams and to legiti-mate human strivings.

Although it is a fine thing to admire sculptures and the well-danced dance, we also need to accept poorly made sculptures and artless dancing. For, "...every gesture which succeeds is made up of all those which fail to hit the mark" (1950, 91). Thus, paying tribute to the well-danced dance does not intend to discourage those who do not dance well. It is, on the contrary, to celebrate the love of dancing per se and so, "The best dances come of a simple zest for dancing; that fervor which insists that everyone, even if he have no skill in dancing, shall join in the dance. Else you have but a joyless, pedantic exercise, an idle show of skill" (1950, 44). This also implies that part of the challenge in praising a job well done is that people come to think that anything but perfection might be scorned or considered insignificant. To open the horizons of significance in one's labors is to begin by understanding that the fervor and zeal of creation is all that ultimately matters. Recalling his father's words, the chieftain advised: "'Build not an empire where everything is perfect...At the core of your perfection will be emptiness, and you shall have no joy of it. Nay, rather build an empire where all is zeal'" (1950, 45).

Review and Synthesis

Items of our world become meaningful when we have willingly torn our flesh in winning them from some resisting force. They also become meaningful when we feel that things are bound in some whole that incorporates them and thus makes them transcend their physical surfaces. They may thereby be rendered meaningful in terms of the magnitude or scope of that whole. But things of the world can become meaningful simply by being drawn away from their opposites, and many items have become meaningful because we place them in light of the goals we see them serving. Finally, many things of our world have histories and are imbued with memories that render them meaningful in terms of the amount of time spent on them.

For further summary, compare the activities and products of painting, sculpting, and writing to acts of dancing, juggling, and singing. In both sets, we find horizons for moving toward perfection, for rejuvenating the world by releasing divinity in the details. All activities, actions, and doings, even everyday speech, can be done in the spirit of a hymn. Moreover, in all, we find horizons for cultivating the individual, fashioning one's talents and capacities. Nevertheless we find a considerable difference between the first set and the second one. Whereas the first set allows material relics and remnants, "Great Works," to be bestowed upon other people and subsequent generations, the second set shows whole domains of action where no product can be bestowed. As de Saint-Exupéry writes, "the well danced dance admits no hoarding." In this way, activities such as found in the second set become a gift of inspiration and can be passed only to those who are able to receive it. *This point cannot be overemphasized*: not all aspects of culture are simply bestowed by other people; much must be earned and then perpetuated, or it vanishes. But we need not choose one set over the other set. We can accept both—linear and cyclical—by realizing that each takes value only by opening to the eternal; each opens in love for the well-done deed.

How, then, are we to give form to the inspiration to create? How are we to release the driving impulse to transcend one's self by placing one's creations in higher esteem than one's personal comforts? Would it even be possible to enable a world where persons everywhere can see their own potential as a creative force, can see the opportunity to thrive and to become?

If we believe, on the contrary, that people seem to be ever becoming more decadent, the solution is difficult: we must help them see the invisible larger whole, and we must be able to show the value of natural resistances and hierarchical impositions. And, about this we must be clear. People who have become sedentary and now sit snugly in their stalls, fluffed up on their moneybags, are not simply to be blamed for leading to the downfall of culture, but rather, their very decadence should be taken as a symptom of their blindness to the whole. De Saint-Exupéry writes:

> A man does not lay down his life for sheep or goats, for dwellings or for mountains...A man lays down his life to preserve the unseen bond which binds them together...And he who has slowly bartered his life for a work well done, which will endure after he is dead—for a temple far outlasting him—such an one is willing enough to die, if his eyes can distinguish the temple from the diversity of materials composing it... (1950, 57-58)

The task, then, is to help people see their daily struggles in terms of the larger wholes of which they are but a part, and much of this chapter has ruminated on strategies and tactics for enabling people to view the unseen knot emanating from the many visible things.

As wisdom is often an attunement to the invisible lines of tensions that generate meaning, this chapter examined de Saint-Exupéry's *The Wisdom of the Sands* to help envision and facilitate a worldview whereby people might maximally enjoy a significant life. When people willingly trade their flesh for some vision of perfection—suffering for an ideal of beauty and grace—they humanize themselves and often inspire others. Fairly recently, a film major from one of the local universities came to my office and asked me if I had seen his flyer and was planning on attending the then upcoming screening of his most recent film. I asked him if his work attempts to beautify the world, if it strives to greatness in heart or deed, if it inspires the uplifting and dignifying in existence, and moreover, if we and the world would be better off because of it? Speechless at first, and a little put off—maybe even slightly insulted—he concluded that I was having him on. In a word, he seemed unable to take seriously the idea of working in those terms.

We need to see how bankrupt and unfulfilling, how utterly uninspiring, is the life of the stall-fed sedentary, the life of the consumerist couch junky. The task is to begin by taming oneself: practice the arts of bartering with absolute vigilance and keep one's temple pure and bright even when there is no inspiration. From this, we unexpectedly discover the grandest of possibilities: living life as if it were an art.

Notes

1   Increasing varieties of mental illnesses such as species of depression and various narcissistic disorders might also be partly the consequences of the increased appeal, the seduction, of the modern individual causa sui project. David K. Reynolds (1983) writes of "Naikan," a Japanese school of psychotherapy, also called the "therapy of indebtedness and gratitude." Naikan, Reynolds tells us, was founded by Ishin Yoshimoto. Yoshimoto believed that the purpose of life is to examine ourselves, and Naikan commonly employs a technique called "Reflection Therapy," where patients are left in a room and told to meditate about people in their lives, starting with their mothers. Patients are to write in every detail from pregnancy up to birth, and then from birth to six months, and then the first year, and so on by responding to the following three questions: 1. What has this person done for me? How has she given to me? 2. What have I done for this person? How have I given back in return? 3. How have I been an inconvenience? How have I been a burden? The explicit goal and common consequence of this therapy is a deep and profound sense of gratitude. One of its many reflection tenets is: "The day you were born was the day your mother suffered" (1995, 279). Summing-up the central meaning of "reflection therapy," Reynolds writes, "I've never met a neurotic filled with gratitude."

2   Saint-Ex never returned from his sixteenth reconnaissance mission. He was reported missing on July 31, 1944.

3   According to one author, "*Citadelle*...grew as he grew and changed as he changed, to which he never saw any real end" (Smith 1956, 229).

4   Around 1992 part of his plane, "The Lightening," was recovered—some forty-two years after he had been reported missing in action. At that time he was commemorated on the fifty franc note. Additionally, a survey was done of the top ten published books in France, the Bible being number one and the works of Saint-Ex filling the remaining nine slots. These were *The Little Prince*, *Night Flight*, and *Wind, Sand and Stars*. *Citadelle*, it should be noted, was not a top ten despite its deep significance for Saint-Ex. In fact, it was mostly abandoned by his readers. At current time, the translation, *WS*, remains out of print.

5   It is only when he, in his fictional tales, meets the Little Prince that someone recognizes his picture as a boa constrictor digesting an elephant. It is also largely for this reason that Saint-Ex tells us that he personally wished to share his life with people who talked about "boa constrictors, or primeval forests, or stars," not people who

would talk only of, "bridge, and golf, and politics, and neckties" (de Saint-Exupéry 1943, 9).

6   Thayer once told students a story of St. Peter's cathedral: A reporter, watching brick-layers set the foundation for St. Peter's cathedral, wished to learn more about the workers and the tasks they were performing. Upon asking one bricklayer the nature of his task, the worker responded, "Can't you see, I am laying bricks." Undiscour-aged, the reporter asked another, to which the second bricklayer responded, "Can't you see, I am building the world's greatest cathedral!" It is the latter worker whom the world now needs most.

7   Cf. Martin Heidegger's "Building Dwelling Thinking" and his "…Poetically Man Dwells…" in *Poetry, Language, Thought*.

8   Becker writes, "Individual unites with group, group with group, and the society as a whole its guiding ideal. In the way the hopeless separation of man from men is over-come; guilt is washed away; the sin of individual burdens of meaning is dispelled. Social aesthetics is, then, the highest possible release of the life force, because it takes place on the level of the whole, integrated community" (1967, 188).

9   For an excellent discussion of these issues see Dorothy Lee's "To Be or Not to Be," from *Valuing the Self*.

10   Marshall McLuhan is known to have suggested that anytime is a good time to live, as long as the society is not changing too quickly.

11   Much has been written about Saint-Ex's scorn for Christianity's tenets regarding the afterlife, its inclinations to pity, and the procrastination of living that he thought those ideas implied (Cate 1970; Migeo 1960; Robinson 1984). He sought a spiritual relationship with the world, but he eschewed values that he believed led people to become too accepting of their lots in life and implicitly urged, at least in his mind, people to become pitiful. Still, Saint-Ex had a strong tendency to intermingle sacred and profane places (also cf. Robinson 1984). He wished for a spiritual relationship that would serve as the fountainhead of fervor in the present life and would give "in-visible to the eye significance" to daily struggles.

"Chaos to thee is order:
In thine eyes
The unloved is lovely,
Who didst harmonize
Things evil with things good,
That there should be
One Word through all things
Everlastingly."
(From Cleanthes's Hymn to Zeus*)*

> *"One who lives*
> *the life of the universe*
> *cannot be much concerned*
> *with his own."*
> *(Santayana, cited in Nussbaum, 1994, 222)*

CHAPTER 6

STOIC VIRTUES AS HEROIC RITUAL PRACTICES

At many points throughout this study I have made reference to neo-Stoicism, and now, in the sixth and final chapter, I turn to its ancient traditions, focusing mainly upon the writings of Epictetus. My goal is to recover some of the resources for expiative-heroism that the Stoics have made available, even if some of their ideas need to be slightly modified for today's world. What the ancient Stoics were able to do, and this study attempts to regain, was to provide a worldview that gives ultimate meaning and significance to all events while avoiding the temptations of the causa sui project. Almost as if anticipating the rise of the modern causa sui project, the ancient Stoics headed it off at the pass. They seemed to grasp the basic heroism that humans most need: humble acts of virtue, the genuine will to do good, and the existential courage of needing little. The heroic expiation explored in this chapter consists, basically, in accepting the ambiguous fact that we are called to strive for harmonious perfection, bartering our all for objects having noble curves and of divine grace, while simultaneously accepting whatever happens as somehow ordained by Divine Providence.

Principles of Order

The Nobel Laureate Octavio Paz, when speaking of language and the poetic possibilities of humanity, once wrote that the gods accidentally left a piece of the creating powers of the universe within one of their creatures. And Kenneth Burke, for his own part in this chorus, writes of human notions of the divine, suggesting that, "even if their ideas of divine perfection were reducible to little more than a language-using animals' ultimate perception of its own linguistic forms, this could be a true inkling of the divine insofar as language itself happened to be made in the image of divinity" (1961, 289-299). These ideas, so concordant with Stoic sensibilities, depict the human situation as conditioned by a Divine Logos; we are, as it were, deities divested of any other powers than those of our action, both practical and symbolic.

But logos, as an ambiguous and endless movement of merger and division, offers people countless opportunities for confusion and delusion. Describing this idea, Stoic scholar George Long writes, "all things are determined by *logos* but the many fail to recognize this and thus seek to organize their lives on alien principles" (1996, 51). Although humans have a portion of the logos and by that right are able to harmonize and resonate with the order all around them, they all-too-often frustrate their lives not only by neglecting what is under their jurisdiction, but also by seeking the impossible: trying to control what is naturally beyond their control. Today, the modern causa sui project encourages precisely this. It is an attempt to make individuals self-sufficient from the bottom-up and thereby to try to circumvent or undercut the fact of natural guilt.

If today's world is mostly caught in the modern causa sui project and is seeking a technological means of absolute control, the ancient Stoics, especially Epictetus,[1] taught a lesson that needs recovery today: one can best minimize and properly handle natural guilt by fundamentally knowing one's proper place. Such a harmonizing begins by learning that it is good to first distinguish between things in our power and things beyond our power and then to align all of our efforts, energies, and concerns into the former, leaving the latter to be within the purview of Providence. Good and evil, by these lights, comes from how we align therein; there is neither good nor evil outside of such alignment.

Neo-Stoic cosmopolitanism most values life's ability to strive toward harmonious perfection; it venerates and pays homage to the harmony of effort and moral intention, and recognizes that greatening one's soul can be offered as a gift to the world and others. In preview, the possibilities of a twin ritual gesture, an expiative-heroism, are given in Stoic life practices such as: extirpating anger, gaining the courage to need little, accepting death, and submitting to cosmic duty. All of these are part of the heroism-expiation whereby persons mortify themselves and, in a kind of transcendence, gain significance by participating in extra-mundane worldly rejuvenation.

Human Reason and Divine Providence

The previous chapter stressed the importance of heritages. It reviewed the ways that the past holds significance for people and the manner in which children, if they are to enjoy this source of significance, need to be taught about who they are in terms of their family origins. They need to learn about their ancestors' struggles and accomplishments and to know something about their family lines. With all of this in mind, we nonetheless need to exercise some caution. For even if all of the above is the case, we still need to recognize and make room for the kind of cosmopolitanism issued by Epictetus where he replied to the question of his origins, stating that he "is a citizen of the world." In a word, we should learn of our family trees and ancestral origins but we should not forget the ambiguity of all this, meaning that all of it becomes a profound lie if taken as overly authoritative. We are in fact children of the universe, fruits of the world, and we belong to it as mountains and trees do. We are indigenous inhabitants. Chapters 2 and 3 have tried to give the framework for sufficiently grasping how all of humanity, each and every person, is suspended in a nexus of particular histories and trajectories but nonetheless related to all that ever has been. We are a part of the grand and absolute mystery. Each and every person, more than from a particular family line, is as much an event of the universe as the universe is itself. As someone who is, you could not have not been; it is only your imagination that allows the fantasy of a world where you never were.

The cosmos pervades all that is, and the eternal is all around us; we are engulfed on all sides, inside and out, by Divine Providence, and virtue consists in aligning one's will accordingly. All life's events, mundane or not, blaze with a divine meaning-horizon if only because Fate ordains that things shall pass as they do. In #31 of the *Enchiridion* of Epictetus, we find him suggesting:

> For piety towards the gods know that the most important thing is this: to have right opinions about them—that they exist, and that they govern the universe well and justly—and to have set yourself to obey them, and to give way to all that happens, following events with a free will, in the belief that they are fulfilled by the highest mind. (1940, 476)

Logos (reason, the human ability to think) is what actually likens humans to the Divine. Although all of life is sacred and permeated by logos, humans gain their distinction by being at the highest location of a phylogenic scale. They are, therefore, not only marked by logos, but they actually have a portion of the logos under their powers. As E. R. Dodds states, "The founder of Stoicism went further still: for Zeno, man's intellect was not merely akin to God, it was God, a portion of the divine substance in its pure or active state" (1951, 238). [2] This idea that the human mind is part of Divine reason is also well articulated in the Harvard Classics collection called the "Golden Sayings of Epictetus" where we find:

> But what saith God?—"Had it been possible, Epictetus, I would have made both that body of thine and thy possessions free and unimpeded, but as it is, be not deceived: —it is not thine own; it is but finely tempered clay. Since then this I could not do, I have given thee a portion of Myself, in the power of desiring and declining and of pursuing and avoiding, and in a word the power of dealing with the things of sense. And if you neglect not this, but place all that thou hast therein, thou shalt never be let or hindered: thou shalt never lament; thou shalt not blame or flatter any. What then? Seemeth this to thee a

little thing?"—God forbid!—"Be content then therewith!" And so I pray the Gods. (1980, 118-119)

And in the writings of Seneca, too, mind is likened to the divine,

> All those objects revered by untutored intellects enslaved to their own bodies—marbles, gold, silver, polished round tables of great size—are earthy dross which an unflawed mind aware of its own nature cannot love,...the mind...is free, kin to the gods, adequate to all space and times, for thought ranges through all heaven and has access to all time, past and future...The mind itself is sacred and everlasting, and not subject to violence. (1958, 123-124)

By stressing that human minds are a "portion of the divine substance" and suggesting that they are "adequate to all space and times," the Stoics recognized humanity as like the gods, somehow, already beyond the confines of visible space.

But here too, we must exercise a great deal of caution, for the Stoics interchangeably slide between and among the words "God," "the gods," "Universal Reason," the "highest mind," "Divine Providence" and even "Fate." Neither monotheism nor polytheism in the modern senses of those words, the neo-Stoicism sketched here likens Divine Providence to neither an individual being nor a consortium of beings. God, or the Divine, is more similar to the necessary principles of balance, harmony, and order that can be witnessed throughout the entire cosmos. The eternality of the Divine is like the eternality of geometry relations rather than like some kind of actual ongoing and everlasting being.[3]

In chapter 3, I roughly outlined a physics for the neo-Stoicism I have been trying to develop. I identified mediation as the universal principle of life: Boundaries are cast such that they temporarily enable indefinitely ongoing events of merger and division, expansion and contraction. Life, in all its forms, is of such self-constant substance; it is ordered in just such a way as to precariously solve, at least for some time, the countless ambiguities that needed to be integrated. To say that life itself was able to solve the ambiguities is to suggest that life *mediates* itself dialectically: Life could not have emerged nor would it continue to be the riddle that it is, if it did its work in only one direction at once. The order all around us, the geometric relations that characterize the body and forms of ontogenetic development, the delicate balance of opposites on countless horizons (day and night, warm and cold, life and death), the many spatial and temporal integrations, are part of the grand mystery, the ambiguous solution to an even more ambiguous set of problems.

Describing a conception of the divine logos that pervades all things, Long writes that "Zeno's account of harmony...makes reference to a 'single and concordant logos' as the ground of harmonious living...what it betokens is evidently something balanced, proportional, ratio-lie" (1996, 207). These recurrent themes of harmony, balance, and proportion suggest a deep recognition that the many different mergers and divisions we experience are all concordant for the highest mind. Pierre Hadot, writing on the ideas of Marcus Aurelius, also provides useful clarification of logos and how it befits both Divine Providence as well as human reason:

> When universal Reason produces world, it engraves certain laws into the coming-into-being of things...the Stoics see the development of the universe as like that of a living being...This theory of the originary impulse corresponds to the idea of an impersonal, immanent providence, within the development of the universe as a whole. The fact that the world is rational does not mean that it is the result of the deliberation, choice, or calculation of some craftsman exterior to his work. Rather, it means that the world possesses its own internal law. (1998, 155-156)

The neo-Stoic position that I am advocating sees the principles of integrity and self-constancy throughout the cosmos. It stresses that we, rather than being a self-cause, always already find ourselves nestled within larger wholes. Human reason is therefore the ability to contemplate on balance, symmetry, harmony, and proportion. We need to learn the principles of who we are, just as we would learn the principles of a circle, triangle, or musical chord. We need to look carefully once again upon the single principle of mediation running throughout the cosmos and to recognize our place within the whole. As Epictetus is said to have suggested, "He who remembers what man is, is discontented at nothing which happens" (Carter's translation of "Fragments," 1957, 300).

Moral Intention and False Beliefs

In the modern world people tend to believe that reason is one kind of process and that the emotions are basically something else. In the Stoic world, and even the ancient world more generally, emotions were recognized as related to cognition and belief; they were not, as in the modern sense, a world separate from thought.

One well-known and ongoing debate of the ancient world between Aristotle, of the Peripatetic school, and Chrysippus, of the Stoic school, hinged precisely on the role of emotions in public and private life. Both schools agreed that passion was a *kind* of reasoning, but the difference boiled down to this: Aristotle recommends studying the use of the passions in rhetoric, stressing the right time and place for the right amount of passion. Emotional responses to unjust events and situations may be the necessary means for bringing about justice, *of course assuming they are tempered and appropriate.*

The Stoics, on the contrary, held that emotions are not needed to perform one's duty, and they also argued that emotions are not as easily controlled as is often implied. This issue is addressed at length in Martha Nussbaum's *The Therapy of Desire* (1994), where she outlines Seneca's concern over the role of anger in public life.[4] People too easily run amuck as they become rallied into an angry mob, and more harm than good comes from anger in public places. But the ancient debate over the role of emotions in public life was not simply over the degree to which anger should be used in motivating people toward action (e.g., the ability to enrage warriors before the battle). Something much more profound is at stake, as Chrysippus taught that *all* emotions were an outcome of having assented to false belief. Thus, if one were able to live as a Stoic Sage, as one who had removed all false beliefs, there simply would be no emotions with which to deal. Now, regardless of whether or not all emotions are, in fact, the result of false beliefs, the neo-Stoicism sketched here would haggle for less. We simply stress that, more often than not, when we feel anger, fear, envy, jealousy, or even basic life-frustration, it is because we have taken under our jurisdiction what is naturally beyond our control.[5] For example, when people get angry we should ask ourselves: what have they imagined as under their control, which naturally is not in their power, but which now blooms into this emotion? What is the assented to false-belief that now gives ground for the emotion? If someone were to walk up to me and spit upon me, my anger comes from assuming that I had some power over what another does. Likewise, if I overhear someone speak wrongly and with condemnation against me, any anger emerges from my assumption that any of this is under my control. Accordingly, we find in Stoicism a wide array of practices and exercises that attempt to extirpate the passions, to reveal false beliefs for what they are. In the *Enchiridion* #20 Epictetus writes, "Remember that foul words or blows in themselves are no outrage, but your judgment that they are so. So when any one makes you angry, know that it is your own thought that has angered you."

I have gone through what might seem to be a digression, but its relevance becomes increasingly apparent as we try to posse up resources for an expiative heroism. Our emotional lives, intricately caught within the drive for significance and worth, can succumb to images of super-fantastical accomplishments in the world, acts of derring-do, where superhuman feats transpire. All of this is a seduction, a glitter and flash of shiny glass. It puts our focus where it should not be and generates emotions as a result. It is a distraction that manufactures an overdrawn ideal of heroism, one that comparatively diminishes the humble, everyday extra-mundane acts that could be called "practicing virtue."

I can further clarify how emotions relate false beliefs and also open a path to a heroism worth wanting, by focusing upon a few representative Stoic ideas in the *Enchiridion* of Epictetus:

> Of all existing things some are in our power, and others are not in our power. In our power are thought, impulse, will to get and will to avoid, and in a word, everything which is our own doing. Things not in our power include the body, property, reputation, office, and, in a word, everything which is not our doing...Make it your study then to confront every harsh impression with the words, "You are but an impression, and not at all what you seem to be." Then test it by those rules that you posses, and first by this—the chief test of all—"Is it concerned with what is in our power or with what is not in our power?" If it is concerned with what is not in our power, be ready with the answer that it is nothing to you. (1940, 468)

So much unnecessary suffering, anguish, and evil comes from either failing to distinguish between things in our power and those that are not, or from failing to stay vigilant in assenting to one's impressions. Other than how we make sense of what is going on, or what we seek to avoid, or what we desire, *and what we actually do*, there is nothing that should be of concern to us.

All that happens outside of the spheres of our powers is neither good nor bad. To these we should be fundamentally indifferent. Well, if not indifferent, we can give a reserved preference, a preference with full and open acceptance of all that happens beyond one's own doing. Whereas Stoic schools taught that some things beyond one's own doing can be preferred even if not necessary, others taught utter indifference to everything beyond one's own doing.[6] Pierre Hadot, in *What is Ancient Philosophy?*, characterizes a neo-Stoic notion of duties by suggesting, "The Stoic always acts 'under reserve': he tells himself, 'I want to do X, if Fate permits.'...but he does act, taking part in social or political life... The Stoic does not act in his own material or even spiritual interest, but acts in a which is always disinterested and in the service of the human community" (1995, 134-135).

The neo-Stoic heroism I am outlining recognizes the *ambiguity* of outcomes and focuses all attention upon the moral intention and follow through. It stresses that whether outcomes are to be preferred or not, these are not, ultimately, under our control. Recall that in chapter 2, we found a common drive toward authoritative disambiguation, a tendency to want to round out the ambiguities of logos in guilt-denying ways. People seem to want it either way: they want to care about and be attached to items outside of their control *or* they want to not even try or exert effort. They seem to think that indifference to outcomes or full acceptance of outcomes is *de facto* license to be indifferent to the effort or any attempt at all. They seem to believe that learning to be indifferent to outcomes and realizing that there is much that is beyond our power necessarily entails, or likely falls into, becoming indifferent to trying. The dual gesture required is a kind of grateful indifference.

The position advanced here confronts this dilemma head-on, taking both horns simultaneously. One way to put these concerns at ease is to see the present moment as a dividing line between past and future, and although the future holds much that is out of our control, there is also a great deal that vitally depends upon our will. The past, on the contrary, is fully out of our control, and it is good to begin by accepting it. On a similar front, people may think to themselves, "why should I act justly to others if they're not just to me?" The answer is as simple as it is obvious: unlike the actions of others, my actions are under my control. There is, perhaps surprisingly, ample evidence from the ancient world that ancient Stoicism was a kind of genetic predecessor to civil rights activism.[7] It is also worth recalling that, unlike the Peripatetic school of Aristotle, the Stoics openly welcomed both women and slaves. In fact, Musonius Rufus, the early teacher of Epictetus, defended the inclusionary practices of the Stoic schools with a paper titled, "That Women Too Should Do Philosophy."[8] And Epictetus maintained that, "Only the educated are free." Admittedly, it is immensely challenging to continuously discern between things in our power and those that are not, and to just as quickly completely give up on assuming control over that which we naturally have no control while simultaneously owning fully all that falls under our jurisdiction. To strive for justice with courage, moderation, and prudence while simultaneously accepting whatever happens (i.e., to be able to do one's best at some project and then not worry about the final product) is a demanding twin gesture. But, in being able to enact this twin gesture, the neo-Stoic hero enables a most potent disambiguation, a vital expiation, one grounded in the power of moral intention.

We can better understand the notion of "moral intention" by carefully considering Epictetus's observation #27: "As a mark is not set up for men to miss it, there is nothing intrinsically evil in the world." This passage well displays the Stoic orientation: the point is to set up your target and aim as best as you can, but you should never fret nor lament about the missed shot nor should you gloat and swell over the shots that hit the mark. Neither the miss nor the hit is ultimately within one's control. But, on the other hand, setting up targets and aiming are both good, for they depend upon us. Evil, on this account, comes from either being indifferent to target setting up or the aiming, or from concerning oneself solely with whether one hits the target or not.

In passage #19 Epictetus writes: "You can be invincible, if you never enter on a contest where victory is not in your power" (1940, 472). As the Stoics often take athletes as their model, Epictetus is not suggesting that people should avoid competitions or games that have winners and losers. Simply do all that is in one's power. As it is beyond one's power how another person performs—the one person whose performance one should be concerned with is one's own. In #29 Epictetus further states,

> You must submit to discipline, eat to order, touch no sweets, train under compulsion, at a fixed hour, in heat and cold, drink no cold water, nor wine, except by order; you must hand yourself over completely to your trainer as you would to a physician, and then when the contest comes you must risk getting hacked, and sometimes dislocating your hand, twist your ankle, swallow plenty of sand, sometimes get of flogging, and will after all this suffer defeat. (1940, 475)

And after all of this, if one is defeated, it is good to see that Destiny has spoken and to dance happily in the Word. It is good to accept what happened. "Hard feelings" come if we take under our control what is fundamentally beyond our control (what and how the others do, even if they cheated or not). If one actually did one's best, owning all that was actually under one's control, one was defeated though remained invincible.

But how might our modern neo-Stoic approach the topic of health and modern medicine? Is not health increasingly under one's control? Certainly our diet, what we choose to eat, and how much we choose to eat are under our control. Also under our control is the amount, if any, that we choose to exercise. But even granting T. S. Eliot's insight that "Most people dig their graves with their teeth," meaning that many life-debilitating diseases are correlated to dietary practices, the actual fate of the body remains beyond our control: Some people are born for muscle building; some are not. Some people have larger frames while others are tiny and frail. Some are born with excellent constitutions while others are sickly and have multiple disabilities. Some people have allergies to countless pollens and irritants; others are subject to hereditary diseases. To these facts of the body, the Stoics give us pretty direct advice. None of these are under our control. They are happenstances of fate and should be nothing to us.

Still, what about recent advances in modern medicine, for example, cosmetic plastic surgery or even a hip or knee replacement? These are difficult questions, especially as the modern causa sui project has become powerful enough to transplant organs and manufacture artificial joints and limbs. These things notwithstanding, the neo-Stoic point would be: perhaps it is preferable to seek means of improving health, but at no point is it, really, under our control. Medicine, we must always remember, is a practice, and even here, some bodies take well to transplants while others do not. For some patients, the outcome of a lumbar laminectomy is paralysis, and not all failed surgical procedures are due to malpractice. There is—and there will remain—much that is beyond our control, and much unnecessary suffering could be alleviated by simply staying vigilant over the distinction between what is under our control and what is not. Drawing a fine line of distinction, Stoic scholar George Long writes,

> Unlike the Aristotelian, who says that successful outcomes make a difference to happiness, the Stoics maintain that they are "preferable" but totally inessential...pursuit of such goals are essential to happiness...Outcomes, to the extent that they fall outside the agents control, are not his business or concern but that of universal nature. (1996, 194)

Long further suggests Stoic schools strictly taught members against the ideas that "...happiness requires us to possess or succeed in implementing any of the things we rationally seek to promote" (1996, 200). Where we barter all that was in our power for a piece of handiwork, a cause, or even an organ transplant, the transcendence we experience comes from the act of giving, not from the completion of the object or the arrival of the intended state of affairs. This means that our informed efforts to be healthy are a good but the sheer fact of health is not.

We moderns in the U.S. have so assented to alien principles. By and large we have accepted authoritative disambiguations that have placed too much under our jurisdiction. As a people most generally, we remain and perhaps have become ever more hypnotized by and aligned with things that are basically outside of our control. Chapter 1 of this study explored how, during the steady degeneration of rituals of rejuvenation and the fairly recent onset of consumer capitalism, self-esteem and heroism became caught within a petty and trivial accumulation of things. As Nussbaum writes, "People often value too many of these external things, or value them too highly, or not enough. Thus they have too much emotion in connection with money, possessions, and reputation, sometimes not enough in connection with the things that are truly worthwhile. An important role for philosophical criticism is to insist on the central role of virtuous action, which can usually be controlled by one's effort" (1994, 96). By focusing upon the moral intention of virtuous action, by focusing on what genuinely is under a person's control, we open the possibility of an extra-mundane heroism.

Virtuous action, I am suggesting, is a genuine heroism, one that incorporates ritual mortification and aligns with a Logos of merger and division that nevertheless lays a cosmic duty on persons. Identifying what he takes as one of Stoicism's most significant features, Burke writes that it found a "way of so merging concepts of servitude and freedom, of obligation and privilege, of obedience and rule, that the free man can be defined in terms of service, and the servant in terms of liberty" (1962, 122). In contrast to a death denial turned into a flight of the war machine or individualist consumer capitalism, we find a cosmic heroism that is not that much to look at from the outside, but, as a twin gesture of expiation and heroism, is precisely the kind of heroism this book has sought to clarify and promote.

Stoic Etiquette

In chapter 4, I drew from the writings of Erving Goffman to show how ritual practices within face-to-face interaction open sources of significance. Although Goffman does not refer to the Stoics in his work, Epictetus gives advice that fits remarkably well with many of the insights and conclusions from chapter 4. Whereas Goffman (1959) is popularly known for having remarked that, "life is a wedding," such an observation was predated by the advice of Epictetus: "Remember that you must behave in life as you would at a banquet. A dish is handed round and comes to you; put out your hand and take it politely. It passes you; do not stop it. It has not reached you; do not be impatient to get it, but wait till your turn comes." Such advice meets the demands of both positive and negative ritual superlatively. To illustrate some of the ritual practices advocated by ancient Stoicism, I quote at length the advice given by Epictetus in entry #33 of *The Handbook*.

> Be silent for the most part, or, if you speak, say only what is necessary and in a few words. Talk, but rarely, if occasion calls you, but do not talk of ordinary things—of gladiators, or horse-races, or athletes, or of meats or drinks— these are topics that arise everywhere—but above all do not talk about men in blame or compliment or comparison...For your body take just so much as your bare needs require, such as food, drink, clothing, house, servants, but cut down all that tends to luxury and outward show. Avoid impurity to the utmost of your power before marriage, and if you indulge your passion, let it be done lawfully. Do not be offensive or censorious to those who indulge it, and do not be always bringing up your own chastity. If someone tells you that so and so speaks ill of you, do not defend yourself against what he says, but answer, "He did not know my other faults, or he would not have mentioned these alone."...In your conversations avoid frequent and disproportionate mention of your own doings or adventures; for other people do not take the same pleasure in hearing what has happened to you as you take in recounting your adventures. (1940, 478-479)

Within this thick description of advice for Stoic manner, demeanor, and interpersonal encounters, we find subtle management of both negative and positive ritual.

Such advice stresses that people know their place in the larger social world and they concern themselves with only what is properly under their jurisdiction.

Stoicism scorns ostentation and impolite behavior, largely because the entire philosophy is geared into life-practices that include duties to the larger communities in which people are imbedded. This spirit of civic duty is nicely summarized by Burke where he contrasts Stoicism to both naturalistic and supernaturalistic philosophies: "Stoic cosmopolitanism was…a state philosophy; and humane, humanistic, in laying its main stress upon *man in society* (rather than upon man in nature or man as a future citizen of heaven)" (1984, 119). Burke rightly identifies the location of Stoic concern as civic.[9] Although Epictetus and Seneca wished students to understand themselves as parts within a larger whole—and that we all have duties to that whole—they also fundamentally convey cosmopolitanism. The whole in question moves all the way up to the entire human community. As Nussbaum suggests, "We are to view ourselves as citizens of the worldwide community of rational beings…we are to regard the political community in which we are placed as a secondary and somewhat artificial matter, our first loyalty and attachment being to the whole" (1994, 343). The Stoic tradition is committed to serving the world broadly or even cosmically construed. It therefore calls for a lean and reserved socially-responsible beneficence.

Indifference to Wealth

In today's capitalistic and consumer culture, products—and in particular products that display pecuniary prowess—are major sign-vehicles for the expression of affluence. Well before luxury became what it is today, early Stoical writing scorned showiness. Much explicitly warns against the accumulation of wealth and the problems of greed and insatiability that arise when individuals come to identify what is outside of themselves as either good or evil. Note that their admonishments are not simply against wealth per say, but more against the idea that anything outside of the will to get and/or reasoning is a good. "You ask then what you can call your own," writes Epictetus. "The answer is—the way you deal with your impressions." Fancy homes, luxury cars, and an endless array of expensive things (technological gadgets), all of these can be more a source of stress and anxiety than of happiness and significance. We need not be against wealth as indifferent to it; it is not, in its own right, a source of significance. If anything we need to caution against those who would teach that wealth is a good.

It is hardly insignificant that two of the most well-known proponents of later Stoicism had radically different stations in life. Epictetus was born a slave and died utterly destitute. Marcus Aurelius, on the other hand, was a wealthy and powerful ruler of Rome. Each found the truth of Stoicism. In fact, Stoicism was thought to be as relevant and useful to Roman statesmen—people of affluence and power—as it was to the common person or the nearly penniless. It is also quite interesting how much of Seneca's writings are relevant today, even though there is a great disparity between the meaning of wealth then and now. Consider a few of Seneca's observations:

> We pass on to property, the greatest source of affliction to humanity. If you balance all our other troubles—death, disease, fears, longings, subjection to labor and pain—with the miseries in which our money involves us, the latter will far outweigh the former....Aren't you ashamed, you who gape at riches? ...Do you think the man who strips himself of Fortune's accessories a pauper or peer of the gods? (1958, 89-90)

Do not many people feel the need to be wrapped up in expensive things and showing jewelry? They may want to have designer name clothing. It is as if they do not have the heroic courage to need little. In his attempt to help his student live a better life, Seneca admonishes Lucilius: "appoint certain days on which you will abandon your routine and become intimate with scarcity...I do not interdict the possession of wealth. But my aim is for you to possess it fearlessly, and this attitude you can achieve only if you are convinced that you can live happily even without wealth" (1958, 180). Seneca suggests that too many people are fooled by their eyes. They believe that happiness comes from material things. As a corrective, he shows how certain practices can enable us to grow indifferent to wealth, shows us how to get a fitting emotional/rational relation to riches.

Becker forcefully revealed the degenerated heroism lodged underneath petty consumer capitalism, and today's modern individualist may be caught within a sense of worth and value based upon things rather than upon cultivated virtue. They may be caught in the hopeless fantasy of having control of what others think of them. But this does not mean that Stoics are without any resources for the differential sense of status and veneration. To respect all people is one thing, but to ask that all people be equally venerated is quite another.[10] Speaking of his criteria for evaluating people, Seneca writes, "I value them not by their jobs but by their character; a man gives himself his own character, accident allots his job" (1958, 194).[11] We find here, once more, a base for the sense of worth, one that is lodged into the domain that is naturally under a person's jurisdiction.

Stoics pursue self-cultivation through knowledge, and, as such, they explicitly align with activities that are ends in their own right. Clarifying this issue, Nussbaum writes, "the art that pursues wisdom has the structure of an art whose activities are (once we reach a sufficiently high level) ends in themselves...like dancing and acting, the art activities are themselves ends...philosophy is not only a road to eudaimonia: practiced at its highest, it is our human end...Phronesis, wise and virtuous thinking, just is eudaimonia" (1994, 366). We find, then, that moral intention and activities of the mind are timeless in that they need not arrive at their goals. They can be *complete* from the very beginning, just as a circle remains a circle no matter its size. Study, dialogue, and wise living, similar to acts of bartering, are ends in themselves and as such they are non-consumptive life-practices. They are heroic expiations, actions and involvements that serve to regenerate the world's resources.

Death Acceptance

Like many philosophical systems in the ancient word, the Stoic tradition makes no lofty bid for an afterlife nor does it instruct us to despise death.[12] Death is outside of one's control, and accordingly, it must be dealt with by indifference. It is accepted as part of the meaning of life, as something that Divine Providence saw to be fitting. The whole of chapter 2 outlined the physics of the cosmos and revealed mortality as one of the necessary implicates in the precarious odyssey of life. In *The Discourses*: book 2, chapter 6, we find Epictetus admonishing us from trying to take under our control what is beyond it: "…know that you are cursing men when you pray for them not to die: it is like a prayer not to be ripened, not to be reaped." And in *The Handbook* #14 he writes, "It is silly to want your children…and your friends to live forever, for that means that you want what is not in your control to be in your control, and what is not yours to be yours" (1940, 471). Not only is the fact of death beyond our control, but, in addition, Providence saw fit that humans can have no knowledge of anything beyond life. We are to act with regard to *this world*, meeting our duties with courage and goodwill and accepting whatever happens.[13] It may well be the case that the more that the "afterlife" becomes the ruling narrative of a person's life, the more that person has assented to alien principles.

As fundamentally beyond our control, death is something to which we should be indifferent, although admittedly the wise may learn how to use death as a resource for gaining perspective and making decisions. In #21 of *The Handbook*, Epictetus advocates a nearness to death, if only to keep desire in its proper place: "Keep before your eyes from day to day death and exile and all things that seem terrible, but death most of all, and then you will never set your thoughts on what is low and will never desire anything beyond measure" (1940, 473). Death too can be regarded as a gift insofar as we can know that we will die, which basically implies that we know that we cannot postpone decisions indefinitely; a time to act will come and then that moment will pass. By maintaining an image of death before us, we are reminded of what is and is not under our control, meaning, essentially, who we really are.[14]

We also find Epictetus giving advice that nicely brings together the Stoic demand of concerning ourselves only with what is under our control while also meeting the demand of social politeness and graciousness. In #16 of *The Handbook*, Epictetus suggests that we can sympathize with someone who is grieving over the loss of a loved one, so long as we remember what it is that actually troubles people:

> When you see a man shedding tears in sorrow for a child abroad or dead, or for loss of property, be sure that you are not carried away by the impression that it is outward ills that make him miserable. Keep this thought to you: "What distresses him is not the event, for that does not distress another, but his judgment on the event." Therefore do not hesitate to sympathize with him as far as words go, and if it so chances, even to groan with him; but take heed that you do not also groan in your inner being. (1940, 472)

Death is not a bad thing. It only seems bad if we already assented to putting under our jurisdiction what is naturally beyond our power. Mortality simply makes sense; it had to come along for life to be what it is, and all of this is good.

Writing about the gift character of existence, Moses Hadas describes Seneca's views on death and death-acceptance. He suggest that once a fully Stoic view is adopted, a person,

> reckons not only his chattels and property and position but even his body and eyes and hand, all that a man cherishes in life, even his own personality, as temporary holdings, and he lives as if he were on loan to himself, and is ready to return the whole sum cheerfully on demand...When the order to return the deposits comes he will not quarrel with Fortune but will say, "I am thankful for what I have held and enjoyed." (1958, 94-95)

It is, in fact, only when we seek what is beyond our control that death becomes an issue. Imagine a spoiled child looking up at the nighttime sky, seeing the stars in the heavens, and the youth reaches up and tries to grab one. Witnessing such an event, a parent might tell the child that this is impossible, "You cannot touch the stars, but you can look at them." We can imagine the child's ungrateful reaction "I don't even want to see what I can't have; I'd just as soon banish the stars." And so, we too may be upset that we can have ideas of what we will never physically experience. Fortunately, we need not life after death, for life itself is enough. We need not hold eternity in our hands. It is enough to merely glimpse eternity, to share in the *logos* and hence to be able to contemplate the Cosmos.

Ultimately, death poses no problem once we focus exclusively upon moral intention rather than ultimate achievement of any ends. Writing on the manner in which moral intention gives an act completeness from its very inception, Pierre

Hadot, writes, "Even if the action which we are carrying out were in fact interrupted by death, this would not make it incomplete; for what gives an action its completeness is precisely the moral intention by which it is inspired, not the subject matter on which it is exercised" (1998, 187). If we have lived right the entire time, all has been good. To live right is to give each day the completeness of the eternal.

Rounding Things Out

What is most important about this study is the way that the contemporary neo-Stoic can effectively accomplished what Becker sought by a "heroism-expiation." These twin impulses, which meet the unfolding of logos, are embodied in habits and practices of virtue: engaging the world and performing duties while bringing oneself into constant harmonious alignment with Fate. Note how this accomplishes both dimensions perfectly.

Moreover, the Stoic worldview accomplishes a horizon of meaning that incorporates indifference. The point throughout has not simply been that many things happen beyond our control and therefore we should simply learn to accept whatever happens. Stoical "indifference" is not the same as modernistic naturalist atheism, which, from within an entirely scientific world-picture, could simply accept life as a kind "accident," a fluke as it were. This is not by any means the neo-Stoic position this book has sought to outline.[15] The Stoic view is that all that happens occurs according to reason, and the task is to accept what happens as a harmony elsewhere enjoyed, to recognize that the order of the world is such that there was no other way. A grateful indifference becomes possible as we diligently distinguish between what is in our power and what is not.

The ability to reason is one of the few things we have under our jurisdiction, one of the only things we do have actual power over. Not only can we learn to accept what is beyond control, but we find that this submission itself is an attunement to divine meaning horizons. We expiate the guilt of being human by our very submission, finding it a challenge to live by such humble virtue, and then, in and through our expiation, we are made ultimately heroic: relieved of a purely human meaning horizon, we become enfolded in the sense that life happens according to a reason. In *The Discourses* Epictetus writes,

> Man, be not ungrateful, nor again forget higher things! Give thanks to God for sight and hearing, yes, and for life itself and what is conducive to life— for grain and fruit, for wine and oil, but remember that He has given you another gift superior to all of these, the faculty which shall use them, test them, and calculate the value of each. (1940, 334)

Life, and all that we enjoy, is a gift, and yet to want our lives and our ultimate fates to be other than they are is to reject the gift (Schrag 2002). It is to fail to realize who we are and how we relate to all that is around us.

The horizons of the neo-Stoic cosmopolitanism, where people practice worldly rejuvenation, are already appearing in the contemporary landscape. Some thinkers who have already started to identify this trend include: Juliet Schor, Morris Berman, Richard Sennett, Albert Borgmann, Alain de Botton, Martha Nussbaum, Naomi Klein, Pierre Hadot, Susan Neiman, and David K. Reynolds. All of these scholars, the trends they identify as well as the traditions they represent, address how slow life, cultivated character and virtue, the courage to need little, and the thoughtfulness of wasting less, are among the richest resources for a significant life. Today's neo-Stoic cosmopolitanites are downsizers and downshifters, people who are choosing a more monistic life, the life of a craftsperson, a life that is other than a corporate logo and a commercial. They are reviving the ancient habits and practices of working with recalcitrant materials, and they are concerned with minimizing the size of footprint they leave in their wake.

The most potent heroism, and the heroism most needed in today's world, is not much to look at. It is not flashy or glamorous. It is extra-mundane to be sure, but mostly in ways that are invisible to the eye. The neo-Stoic heroism of worldly rejuvenation is nothing more and nothing less than the humble act of always accepting everything that comes to pass yet nevertheless continuing to seek justice and to perform one's social and cosmic duties to the best of one's ability. It sounds so simple. The point is obvious. But anyone who has tried to stay vigilant in accepting what happens while striving to the best of one's ability knows how absolutely demanding and genuinely heroic it is.

Notes

1   Epictetus, born around 55 AD., was a slave of the tyrant Epaphroditus as well as a pupil of the Stoic teacher Musonius Rufus. Legend holds that one day Epaphroditus was tugging and twisting the leg of Epictetus who, at a certain point, turned and warned, "If you twist any further you will break it." When it broke, Epictetus retorted, "See, I told you you would break it." Eventually, as lamed and grown learned in Stoicism, he was freed and began to teach Stoic philosophy in Rome and then in Greece. Around 100 AD his most well known student, Arrian, composed the lecture notes now known as *The Discourses*. These, along with the *Enchiridion* (or *The Handbook*), are his most well-known and studied texts. In his personal life, Epictetus lived alone with very few possessions, and then, later in life, he cohabitated with a woman and they adopted a sickly boy.

2   Thus Seneca in his *Epistles* can write: "Call boldly upon God: you will not be asking him for that which belong to another" (2002, 59).

3   If there is any such being, it is the Sun, and it is to the Sun that we all eventually will return.

4 It is interesting to note that, although Seneca is critical of anger in public life, he also writes, in his *Epistles*, "More murderers speculate on their profits than give vent to hatred" (2003, 89)

5 Chrysippus admittedly may have overstated his argument. There seems to be, as Plato would remind us, a line that divides the "courageous" from the "foolhardy." Point well taken, but the two points to be underscored here are first the relation between emotion and cognition, and second the point that many emotions do come from false beliefs and that these can be extirpated. Perhaps the richest source here is Bakhtin (1993).

6 See Long's *Stoic Studies* (1996).

7 Cf. Nussbaum (1994); Hadot (1995).

8 See Nusbaum (1994).

9 Burke suggests that the Stoics counter the prevailing taxonomies of the human, which were human is an organism in an environment and human is a soul awaiting other-worldly membership, by suggesting that the human is a social creature per se, and sociopolitical one. Today, this has mostly eroded and the two modes of definition have come to prevail. The dominant motive schemes become science and religion, both of which can fall into the individual causa sui project, the scientific by technological innovation, and the religious by pious observances. It is interesting to speculate that literacy and money were the two forces of logos that made possible the individual causa sui project, and so, both religion and science cut against the highly sociopolitical obligation model of Stoicism toward an individualist program of life (either a scientific orientation toward the body per se, and the religious focus on *personal* salvation).

10 Without a doubt, one of the most interesting characters in the ancient world is Socrates. If Lee Thayer is correct in suggesting that only the great masters succeed in being ambiguous, Socrates was indeed a great master. He is not only claimed as founding inspiration by Plato and his Academy, but equally by the Stoics and the Cynics. In fact, Diogenes the dog, known as "Little Socrates," was more in demeanor and lifestyle similar to Socrates than was Plato.

11 As Nussbaum suggests, "The Stoics frequently…criticize the differential treatment of human beings based on superficial distinctions of status, class, origin, gender, wealth" (1994, 334).

12 Elizabeth Carter, in her introduction to *Moral Discourses, Enchiridion and Fragments*, writes, "There is, I think, very little evidence to be found that they (the Stoics) believed future rewards or punishments, compared with that which appears to the contrary…Epictetus never asserts either. He strongly insists that a bad man hath no other punishment that being such; and a good man no other reward" (1957, xiv).

13 Hans Jonas writes, "In Stoicism, Man provided this end by possession of reason, which makes him the culmination of a terrestrial scale of being that is also self-justifying throughout all its grades (the end as the best of many that are good in degrees); in Christianity, by his possession of an immortal soul, which makes him the sole *imago Dei* in creation (the end as the sole issue at stake); and Cartesian dualism radicalized this latter position by making even sole possessor of inwardness or 'soul' of any kind, thus the only one of whom 'end' can meaningfully be predicated as he alone can entertain ends. All other life, the product of physical necessity, can be considered his means" (1966, 60).

14 Each of us is, Epictetus writes, "a tiny soul carrying around a corpse."

15 Hadot again: "Stoic indifference is profoundly different from Skeptic indifference...
    For the Stoic...indifference consists in making no differences, but in equally want-
    ing—and even equally loving—everything that is willed by Fate" (2002, 133).

"…mankind's only hope is a cult of comedy." (The cult of tragedy is too eager to help out with the holocaust. And in the last analysis it is too pretentious to allow for the proper recognition of our animality.) (Burke 1966, 20)

"Let us,
in the spirit of solemn comedy,
... be on guard
...as regards the subtleties of sacrifice,
in their fundamental relationship
to governance."
(Burke 1961, 235)

EPILOGUE

ON COMIC CORRECTIVES

Joseph Campbell's *The Power of Myth* tells the story of the "Face of Glory," a tale he learned from Heinrich Zimmer's *Myths and Symbols in Indian Art and Civilization.* Apparently, one day while Shiva was on the throne, Rahu, a demon sent by Jalandhara, came to steal Shiva's goddess bride Shakti. In response to this affront, Shiva blasts energy from the spot between the eyebrows ("The Lotus of Command") and conjures a hungry lion-headed demon. The demon roared, and Rahu, aghast with fright but savvy in the way of diplomacy and negotiation, begged for forgiveness. With great benevolence, Shiva spared Rahu's life. But the lion-headed demon howled its hunger pains more loudly than ever. Shiva, faced with this difficulty but well understanding the hunger of conjured beasts, suggested that the lion-headed demon consume itself. And so it proceeded. The monster began with its feet, and, in blind voraciousness, devoured more and more of its own flesh. Shiva felt deep kinship with this nightmarish procedure and felt gratified by witnessing such a vivid manifestation of self-consuming power. Zimmer concludes the myth by suggesting that Shiva "smiled upon that creature of his wrath—which had reduced its own body, joint by joint, to the nothingness of only a face—benignantly declared 'You will be known, henceforth, as "Face of Glory" (*kirttimukha*), and I ordain that you shall abide forever at my door. Whoever neglects to worship you shall never win my grace'" (Zimmer 1946, 175-182).

We find a gentler version of the all one self-consuming mystery in the wonderful little book, *The Book: On The Taboo Against Knowing Who You Are,* where Alan Watts suggests a cosmology that might be well expressed as a cocktail-party version of Hinduism. He writes that in the beginning there was one and only one thing, and then the thing cried out: "I am lonely." Then, it divided itself in half. Both sides simultaneously looked at the other side and both sides simultaneously said. "Oh, now I'm bored." And then one side turned black and the other side turned white, and the mystery of this difference made one say, "What is that?"

And the other side, startled and fascinated by what it was seeing and hearing, replied, "who said that?" Then—with the creative impulse of mystery and sublimated difference—the two exploded into endless varieties of beings and relations. Clouds, flowers, plants, animals, and people, everything we can touch, see, and encounter. All of these are instances of the ONE playing a cosmic game of hide and seek upon itself, all so that it need not be eternally lonely and bored. Watts further tells us that, knowing what we now know, there is nothing left to do but laugh. What are we to do but laugh and go on from there.

G. K. Chesterton is known to have said: "Angels can fly because they take themselves so lightly." Likewise, the very heavy ideas Becker, Saint-Exupéry, and Epictetus should not drown us in "spirit of seriousness." Laughter and comedy are vital expressions of our deepest sense of life, and so what could be more fitting than ending with, as Burke suggests, a "comic corrective"? Laughter, *especially at ourselves*, may be a mode of guilt expiation and forgiveness that people cannot do without. Nietzsche helps people dance to these comical tunes:

> Who among you can at the same time laugh and be exalted...

> And to me also, who appreciate life, the butterflies, and soap-bubbles, and whatever is like them amongst us, seem most to enjoy happiness.

> To see these light, foolish, pretty, lively little sprites flit about—that moveth Zarathustra to tears and song.

> I should only believe in a God that would know how to dance.

> And when I saw my devil, I found him serious, thorough, profound, solemn: he was the spirit of gravity—through him all things fall.

> Not by wrath, but by laughter, do we slay. Come, let us slay the spirit of gravity! (1954, 40-41).

I cannot help but give Susanne K. Langer the final word of this book, for she helps us laugh at our gloriously humble (or is that humbly glorious?) place in existence. She writes, citing J. M. Thorburn: "All the genuine, deep delight of life is in showing people the mud-pies you have made; and life is at its best when we confidingly recommend our mud-pies to each other's sympathetic consideration" (1942, iii).

Appendix B

Dogma Be Damned

Silent interlocutor
In whose name we speak
Give us the courage to speak
Despite your lack of response

Foregoing all dogma
But feeling so clearly the mystery engulfing us
The mystery that we too are
I know that I am not alone

There is no aloneness

To speak is to dwell
In the love of the unknown other
A love beyond many generations

Give us strength mysterious ground
Help us come to terms
With your eternal silence
Let our duty be
To faithfully speak your will

Dogma be Damned
I need no false miracles
Life itself is enough

No virgin births
No afterlife
No ultimate recompense

No figure in the sky
No doer of deeds
No granter of mercy
And, no grand adjudicator

I need nothing more
Than what I already have

Life itself

Life is the miracle
And the miracle is us
Trees, rain, and wind
Sun, moon, and sky
These are our sacred texts
Let regain the ancient literacy
Help us read the logos
Inscribed throughout the cosmos

Harmony and order
Growth and change
Variety, variety, variety

The mystery is all around us
And we too are the mystery
For we remain mysterious
Even to ourselves

Oh silent interlocutor
The relation of our self-relation
You are the only conscience
The world can ever have
Help us speak faithfully
To the whole of our being

May our many prayers
Of gratitude and forgiveness
Our prayers for strength and courage
Be neither heard nor responded to
May they harmoniously resonate
With the sacred majesty
Of the self-aware cosmos

Earth you are my Mother
I am your offspring and your caretaker
Help me remember
Who I really am

C.A.

WORKS CITED

Ames, A. Jr. 1960. *The Morning Notes of Adelbert Ames Jr.* New Brunswick, NJ: Rutgers University Press.

Anton, C. 1999. Beyond the Constitutive/Representational Dichotomy: The Phenomenological Notion of Intentionality. *Communication Theory 9*: 26-57.

———. 2001. *Selfhood and Authenticity.* Albany, NY: SUNY Press.

———. 2003. Playing With Bateson: Denotation, logical types, and analog and digital communication. *The American Journal of Semiotics 19* (1-4): 129-154.

———. 2006. Dreamless Sleep and the Whole of Human Life: An ontological exposition. *Human Studies: A Journal for Philosophy and the Social Sciences 29* (2): 181-202.

———. 2007. On the Nonlinearity of Human Communication: Insatiability, context, form. *The Atlantic Journal of Communication 15* (2): 79-102.

———. 2008. Agency and Efficacy in Interpersonal Communication: Particularity as Once-Occurrence and Non-Interchangeability. *The Atlantic Journal of Communication, 16* (3/4): 164-183.

———. 2010. Ethicality, Morality, and Legality: Alignments of speech, writing, and print respectively. *Valuation and Media Ecology: Ethics, Morals, and Laws.* Ed. C. Anton. Cresskill, NJ: Hampton Press.

Bakhtin, M. M. 1993. *Toward a Philosophy of the Act.* Trans. V. Liapunov. Austin, TX: University of Texas Press.

Bateson, G. 1972. *Steps to an Ecology of Mind.* New York: Ballantine Books.

Becker, E. 1967. *Beyond Alienation.* New York: George Braziller.

———. 1969. *Angel in Armor.* New York: George Braziller.

———. 1971a. *The Birth and Death of Meaning.* New York: The Free Press.

———. 1971b. *The Lost Science of Man.* New York: George Braziller.

———. 1973. *The Denial of Death.* New York: The Free Press.

———. 1975. *Escape From Evil.* New York: The Free Press.

———. 2005. The Spectrum of Loneliness. *The Ernest Becker Reader*. Ed. D. Liechty. Seattle, WA: University of Washington Press.

Bleibtreu, J. N. 1968. *The Parable of the Beast*. New York: Macmillan.

Brown, N. O. 1985. *Life Against Death*. Middleton, CN: Wesleyan University Press.

Burke, K. 1952. *A Grammar of Motives*. New York: Prentice-Hall.

———. 1954. *Permanence and Change*. Indianapolis: The Bobbs-Merrill Company.

———. 1957. *The Philosophy of Literary Form*. Berkeley, CA: University of California Press.

———. 1961. *The Rhetoric of Religion*. Berkeley, CA: University of California Press.

———. 1962. *A Grammar of Motives and A Rhetoric of Motives*. New York: The World Publishing Co.

———. 1966. *Language as Symbolic Action*. Berkeley, CA: University of California Press.

———. 1982. *Towards a Better Life*. Berkeley, CA: University of California Press.

———. 1984. *Attitudes Toward History*. Berkeley, CA: University of California Press.

Cassirer, E. 1944. *An Essay on Man*. New Haven, CN: Yale University Press.

Cate, C. 1970. *Antoine de Saint-Exupéry: His life and times*. New York: G. P. Putnam's Sons.

Crable, B. 2009. *Distance as Ultimate Motive: A Dialectical Interpretation of A Rhetoric of Motives, 39* (3): 213-239.

de Saint-Exupéry, A. 1943. *The Little Prince*. Trans. K. Woods. New York: Reynal & Hitchcock.

———. 1965. *A Sense of Life*. Trans. A. Foulke. New York: Funk & Wagnalls.

———. 1950. *The Wisdom of the Sands*. Trans. S. Gilbert. New York: Harcourt, Brace and Company.

Dennett, D. C. 1984. *Elbow Room*. Cambridge, MA: The MIT Press.

Dewey, J. 1988. *The Later Works of John Dewey, 1925-1953. Vol. 1: 1925. Experience and Nature*. Carbondale, IL: Southern Illinois University Press.

Dodds, E. R. 1951. *The Greeks and the Irrational*. Berkeley, CA: University of California Press.

Dubos, R. 1968. *So Human an Animal*. New York: Charles Scribner's Sons.

Duncan, H. D. 1962. *Communication and Social Order*. New York: The Bedminster Press.

Epictetus. 1957. *Moral Discourses, Enchiridion and Fragments*. Trans. E. Carter. New York: E. P. Dutton and Co.

———. 1940. The Discourses of Epictetus. *The Stoic and Epicurean Philosophers: The complete extant writings of Epicurus, Epictetus, Lucretius, Marcus Aurelius*. Ed. W. J. Oates. New York: Random House.

———. 1980. The Golden Saying of Epictetus. *Harvard Classics: Plato, Epictetus, Marcus Aurelius*. Ed. C. W. Eliot. Danbury, CT: Grolier Enterprises Corp.

Gabor, D. 1972. *The Mature Society*. New York: Praeger Publishers.

Goffman, E. 1959. *The Presentation of Self in Everyday Life*. New York: Doubleday Anchor Books.

———. 1961a. *Asylums: Essays on the Social Situation of Mental Patients and Other Innmates*. Garden City: Anchor Books.

———. 1961b. *Encounters: Two Studies in the Sociology of Interaction*. Indianapolis: Bobbs-Merrill Co.

———. 1963a. *Behavior in Public Places: Notes on the Social Organization of Gatherings*. New York: The Free Press.

———. 1963b. *Stigma: Notes on the Management of Spoiled Identity*. New York: Touchstone Books.

———. 1967. *Interaction Ritual: Essays on Face-to-Face Behavior*. New York: Pantheon Books.

———. 1969. *Strategic Interaction*. Philadelphia: University of Pennsylvania Press.

———. 1971. *Relations in Public: Microstudies of the Public Order*. New York: Basic Books.

———. 1974. *Frame Analysis: An Essay On the Organization of Experience*. Boston: Northeastern University Press.

———. 1981. *Forms of Talk*. Philadelphia: University of Pennsylvania Press.

Hadot, P. 1995. *Philosophy as a Way of Life*. Trans. M. Chase. Oxford: Oxford University Press.

———. 1998. *The Inner Citadel: The Meditations of Marcus Aurelius*. Trans. M Chase. Cambridge, MA: Harvard University Press.

———. 2002. *What is Ancient Philosophy?* Trans. M. Chase. Cambridge, MA: Harvard University Press.

Harding, D. E. 1981. On Having No Head. *The Mind's I: Fantasies and reflections on self and soul*. Eds. D. R. Hofstadter and D. C. Dennett. New York: Basic Books.

Heidegger, M. 1984. *The Metaphysical Foundations of Logic*. Trans. M. Heim. Bloomington, IN: Indiana University Press.

———. 1993. *The Concept of Time*. Trans. W. McNeill. Cambridge, MA: Blackwell Publishers.

———. 1995. *The Fundamental Concepts of Metaphysics*. Trans. W. McNeill and N. Walker. Bloomington, IN: Indiana University Press.

———. 1997. *Being and Time*. Trans. J. Stambaugh. Albany, NY: SUNY Press.

Herder, J. G. 1966. *Essay on the Origin of Language*. Trans. A. Gode. Chicago: University of Chicago Press.

Hoffer, E. 1951. *The True Believer*. New York: Harper & Row Publishing.

———. 1976. *In Our Time*. New York: Harper and Row Publishing.

Hyde, L. 1983. *The Gift*. New York: Random House.

Ivins, W. 1969. *Prints and Visual Communication*. Cambridge, MA: The MIT. Press.

Jonas, H. 1958. *The Gnostic Religion: The message of the alien God and the beginnings of Christianity*. Boston: Beacon Press.

———. 1966. *The Phenomenon of Life*. Chicago: The University of Chicago Press.

———. 1996. *Mortality and Morality*. Ed. Lawrence Vogel. Evanston, IL: Northwestern University Press.

Kahnler, E. 1956. *Man The Measure*. New York: George Braziller.

Keller, H. 1904. *The Story of My Life*. New York: Doubleday, Page and Company.

Kenny, R. W. 2000. The Constitutional Dialectic. *Quarterly Journal of Speech 86*: 455-464.

Kierkegaard, S. 1992. *Concluding Unscientific Postscript to Philosophical Fragments*. Trans. H. V. Hong and E.H. Hong. Princeton, NJ: Princeton University Press.

Koestler, A. 1967. *The Ghost in the Machine*. London: Pan Books.

Laertius, D. 1991. *Lives of Eminent Philosophers*. 2 vols. Trans. R. D. Hicks. Cambridge, MA: Harvard University Press.

Laing, R. D. 1990. Confirmation and Disconfirmation. *Self and Others*. New York: Penguin Books.

Langer, S. K. 1942. *Philosophy in a New Key: A study in the symbolism of reason, rite and art*. New York: Mentor Books.

Leder, D. 1990. *The Absent Body*. Chicago: The University of Chicago Press.

Lee, D. 1976. To Be or Not to Be. *Valuing the Self*. Prospect Heights, IL: Waveland Press.

Liechty, D. 2005. *The Ernest Becker Reader*, Ed. Seattle: University of Washington Press.

Lingis, A. 1994. *The Community of Those Who Have Nothing In Common*. Bloomington, IN: Indiana University Press.

Long, A. A. 1996. *Stoic Studies*. Berkeley, CA: University of California Press.

McLuhan, M. 1964. *Understanding Media: Extensions of Man*. Cambridge, MA: The MIT Press.

———, and Mcluhan, E. 1988. *Laws of Media: The New Science*. Toronto: University of Toronto Press.

———. 1969. *Counterblast*. New York: Harcourt, Brace & World, Inc.

Merleau-Ponty, M. 1973. *The Prose of the World*. Trans. J. O'Neill. Evanston, IL: Northwestern University Press.

———. 1962. *Phenomenology of Perception*. Trans. C. Smith. Atlantic Highlands, NJ: The Humanities Press.

Migeo, M. 1960. *Saint-Exupéry*. New York: McGraw-Hill Book Company, Inc.

Miner, H. 1956. The Body Ritual Among the Nacirema. *American Anthropologist* 59: 503-507.

Needleman, J. 1994. *Money and the Meaning of Life*. New York: Doubleday Books.

Nietzsche, F. 1954. *Thus Spake Zarathustra*. Trans. T. Common. New York: The Modern Library.

———. 1968. *The Genealogy of Morals* in *Basic Writing of Nietzsche*. Trans. W. Kaufmann. New York: The Modern Library.

———. 1974. *The Gay Science*. Trans. W. Kaufmann. New York: Vantage Books.

Nussbaum, M. 1994. *The Therapy of Desire: Theory and Practice in Hellenistic Ethics*. Princeton, NJ: Princeton University Press.

Oates, W. J. 1940. *The Stoic and Epicurean Philosophers: The complete extant writings of Epicurus, Epictetus, Lucretius, Marcus Aurelius*. New York: Random House.

Olson, D. 1994. *The World on Paper*. Oxford: Oxford University Press.

Ong, W. J. 1967. *The Presence of the Word*. New York: Simon and Schuster.

———. 1984. Orality, Literacy, and Medieval Textualization. *New Literary History 16*: 1-12.

———. (1986). *Hopkins, the Self, and God*. Toronto: University of Toronto Press.

———. 1992-1999. *Faith and Contexts*. 4 vols. Eds. Thomas J. Farrell and Paul A. Soukup. Atlanta: Scholars Press. (Now distributed by Rowman & Littlefield.)

Ortega y Gasset, J. 1956. In Search of Goethe from Within. *The Dehumanization of Art*. Garden City, NY: Anchor Books.

Percy, W. 1954. *The Message in the Bottle: How Queer Man Is, How Queer Language Is, and What One Has to Do With the Other*. New York: Farrar, Straus and Giroux.

———. 1983. *Lost in the Cosmos: The Last Self-Help Book*. New York: Farrar, Straus and Giroux.

Reynolds, D. K. 1983. *Nakian Psychotherapy: Meditation for Self-Development*. Chicago: University of Chicago Press.

———. 1995. *A Handbook for Constructive Living*. New York: William Morrow and Co.

Robinson, Joy, D. 1984. *Antoine de Saint-Exupéry*. Boston: Twayne Publishers.

Sartre, J. P. 1956. *Being and Nothingness*. Trans. H. E. Barnes. Avenel, NJ: Gramercy Books.

Saunders. J. L. 1966. *Greek and Roman Philosophy After Aristotle*. New York: The Free Press.

Scheler, M. 1961. *Man's Place in Nature*. Trans. H. Meyerhoff. New York: The Noonday Press.

Schrag, C. O. 2002. *God as Otherwise than Being: Toward A Semantics of the Gift*. Evanston, IL: Northwestern University Press.

Seneca. 1917. *Ad Lucilium Epistulae Morales*. 3 vols. Trans. R. M. Gummere. Cambridge, MA: Harvard University Press.

———. 1958. *The Stoic Philosophy of Seneca*. Trans. M. Hadas. New York: W.W. Norton & Company.

———. 2002. *Epistles 1-65*. Trans. R. M. Gummere. Cambridge, MA: Harvard University Press.

Shah, I. 1978. *Learning to Learn: Psychology and Spirituality the Sufi Way*. San Francisco, CA: Harper and Row.

Simmel, G. 1978. *The Philosophy of Money*. Trans. T. Bottomore and D. Frisby. New York: Routledge.

Smith, M. 1956. *Knight of the Air*. New York: Pageant Press.

Stahmer, H. 1968. *Speak! That I May See Thee!* New York: The Macmillan Company.

Straus, E. 1963. *Primary World of the Senses*. New York: Free Press of Glencoe.

———. 1966, *Phenomenological Psychology*. Trans. E. Eng. New York: Basic Books.

Taylor, C. 1995. *Philosophical Arguments*. Cambridge, MA: Harvard University Press.

Thayer, L. 1987. *On Communication*. Norwood, NJ: Ablex Publishing.

————. 1988. Leadership/Communication: A critical review and a modest proposal. *Handbook of Organizational Communication*. Ed. G. Goldhaber. Norwood, NJ: Ablex Press.

————. 1997. *Pieces: Toward a Revisioning of Communication/Life*. Norwood, NJ: Ablex Press.

Veblen, T. 1899. *The Theory of the Leisure Class*. New York: The Modern Library.

von Uexküll, J. 1926. *Theoretical Biology*. New York: Harcourt, Brace and Co.

Watts, A. 1966. *The Book: On the taboo against knowing who you are*. New York: Vintage Books.

————. 1968. *Does It Matter?* New York: Vintage Books.

Watzlawick, P. 1976. *How Real is Real?: Confusion, Disinformation, and Communiction*. New York: Vantage Books.

Zimmer, H. 1946. *Myths and Symbols in Indian Art and Civilization*. New York: Harper & Row.

INDEX